EACL Workshop on Computational Linguistic Aspects of Grammatical Interface 2009

(CLAGI 2009)

Held in Conjunction with EACL 2009

Athens, Greece
30 March 2009

ISBN: 978-1-61738-561-2

Printed from e-media with permission by:

Curran Associates, Inc.
57 Morehouse Lane
Red Hook, NY 12571
www.proceedings.com

Some format issues inherent in the e-media version may also appear in this print version.

Printed by Curran Associates, Inc. (2010)

Association for Computational Linguistics
209 N. Eighth Street
Stroudsburg, Pennsylvania 18360

Phone: 1-570-476-8006
Fax: 1-570-476-0860

acl@aclweb.org

Preface

We are delighted to present you with this volume containing the papers accepted for presentation at the 1st workshop CLAGI 2009, held in Athens, Greece, on March 30th 2009.

We want to acknowledge the help of the PASCAL 2 network of excellence.

Thanks also to Damir Ćavar for giving an invited talk and to the programme committee for the reviewing and advising.

We are indebted to the general chair of EACL 2009, Alex Lascarides, to the publication chairs, Kemal Oflazer and David Schlangen, and to the Workshop chairs Stephen Clark and Miriam Butt, for all their help. We are also grateful for Thierry Murgue's assistance when putting together the proceedings.

Wishing you a very enjoyable time at CLAGI 2009!

Menno van Zaanen and Colin de la Higuera
CLAGI 2009 Programme Chairs

CLAGI 2009 Program Committee

Program Chairs:

Menno van Zaanen, Tilburg University (The Netherlands)
Colin de la Higuera, University of Saint-Étienne, (France)

Program Committee Members:

Pieter Adriaans, University of Amsterdam (The Netherlands)
Srinivas Bangalore, AT&T Labs-Research (USA)
Leonor Becerra-Bonache, Yale University (USA)
Rens Bod, University of Amsterdam (The Netherlands)
Antal van den Bosch, Tilburg University (The Netherlands)
Alexander Clark, Royal Halloway, University of London (UK)
Walter Daelemans, University of Antwerp (Belgium)
Shimon Edelman, Cornell University (USA)
Jeroen Geertzen, University of Cambridge (UK)
Jeffrey Heinz, University of Delaware (USA)
Colin de la Higuera, University of Saint-Étienne (France)
Alfons Juan, Polytechnic University of Valencia (Spain)
Frantisek Mraz, Charles University (Czech Republic)
Georgios Petasis, National Centre for Scientific Research (NCSR) "Demokritos" (Greece)
Khalil Sima'an, University of Amsterdam (The Netherlands)
Richard Sproat, University of Illinois at Urbana-Champaign (USA)
Menno van Zaanen, Tilburg University (The Netherlands)
Willem Zuidema, University of Amsterdam (The Netherlands)

Table of Contents

Grammatical Inference and Computational Linguistics

Menno van Zaanen
Tilburg Centre for Creative Computing
Tilburg University
Tilburg, The Netherlands
mvzaanen@uvt.nl

Colin de la Higuera
University of Saint-Étienne
France
cdlh@univ-st-etienne.fr

1 Grammatical inference and its links to natural language processing

When dealing with language, (machine) learning can take many different faces, of which the most important are those concerned with learning languages and grammars from data. Questions in this context have been at the intersection of the fields of inductive inference and computational linguistics for the past fifty years. To go back to the pioneering work, Chomsky (1955; 1957) and Solomonoff (1960; 1964) were interested, for very different reasons, in systems or programs that could deduce a language when presented information about it.

Gold (1967; 1978) proposed a little later a unifying paradigm called identification in the limit, and the term of grammatical inference seems to have appeared in Horning's PhD thesis (1969).

Out of the scope of linguistics, researchers and engineers dealing with pattern recognition, under the impulsion of Fu (1974; 1975), invented algorithms and studied subclasses of languages and grammars from the point of view of what could or could not be learned.

Researchers in machine learning tackled related problems (the most famous being that of inferring a deterministic finite automaton, given examples and counter-examples of strings). Angluin (1978; 1980; 1981; 1982; 1987) introduced the important setting of active learning, or learning for queries, whereas Pitt and his colleagues (1988; 1989; 1993) gave several complexity inspired results with which the hardness of the different learning problems was exposed.

Researchers working in more applied areas, such as computational biology, also deal with strings. A number of researchers from that field worked on learning grammars or automata from string data (Brazma and Cerans, 1994; Brazma, 1997; Brazma et al., 1998). Similarly, stemming from computational linguistics, one can point out the work relating language learning with more complex grammatical formalisms (Kanazawa, 1998), the more statistical approaches based on building language models (Goodman, 2001), or the different systems introduced to automatically build grammars from sentences (van Zaanen, 2000; Adriaans and Vervoort, 2002). Surveys of related work in specific fields can also be found (Natarajan, 1991; Kearns and Vazirani, 1994; Sakakibara, 1997; Adriaans and van Zaanen, 2004; de la Higuera, 2005; Wolf, 2006).

2 Meeting points between grammatical inference and natural language processing

Grammatical inference scientists belong to a number of larger communities: machine learning (with special emphasis on inductive inference), computational linguistics, pattern recognition (within the structural and syntactic sub-group). There is a specific conference called ICGI (*International Colloquium on Grammatical Inference*) devoted to the subject. These conferences have been held at Alicante (Carrasco and Oncina, 1994), Montpellier (Miclet and de la Higuera, 1996), Ames (Honavar and Slutski, 1998), Lisbon (de Oliveira, 2000), Amsterdam (Adriaans et al., 2002), Athens (Paliouras and Sakakibara, 2004), Tokyo (Sakakibara et al., 2006) and Saint-Malo (Clark et al., 2008). In the proceedings of this event it is possible to find a number of technical papers. Within this context, there has been a growing trend towards problems of language learning in the field of computational linguistics.

The formal objects in common between the two communities are the different types of automata and grammars. Therefore, another meeting point between these communities has been the different workshops, conferences and journals that focus on grammars and automata, for instance,

Proceedings of the EACL 2009 Workshop on Computational Linguistic Aspects of Grammatical Inference, pages 1–4,
Athens, Greece, 30 March 2009.

FSMNLP, GRAMMARS, CIAA, ...

3 Goal for the workshop

There has been growing interest over the last few years in learning grammars from natural language text (and structured or semi-structured text). The family of techniques enabling such learning is usually called "grammatical inference" or "grammar induction".

The field of grammatical inference is often subdivided into formal grammatical inference, where researchers aim to proof efficient learnability of classes of grammars, and empirical grammatical inference, where the aim is to learn structure from data. In this case the existence of an underlying grammar is just regarded as a hypothesis and what is sought is to better describe the language through some automatically learned rules.

Both formal and empirical grammatical inference have been linked with (computational) linguistics. Formal learnability of grammars has been used in discussions on how people learn language. Some people mention proofs of (non-)learnability of certain classes of grammars as arguments in the empiricist/nativist discussion. On the more practical side, empirical systems that learn grammars have been applied to natural language. Instead of proving whether classes of grammars can be learnt, the aim here is to provide practical learning systems that automatically introduce structure in language. Example fields where initial research has been done are syntactic parsing, morphological analysis of words, and bilingual modelling (or machine translation).

This workshop organized at EACL 2009 aimed to explore the state-of-the-art in these topics. In particular, we aimed at bringing formal and empirical grammatical inference researchers closer together with researchers in the field of computational linguistics.

The topics put forward were to cover research on all aspects of grammatical inference in relation to natural language (such as, syntax, semantics, morphology, phonology, phonetics), including, but not limited to

- Automatic grammar engineering, including, for example,
  - parser construction,
  - parameter estimation,
  - smoothing, ...
- Unsupervised parsing
- Language modelling
- Transducers, for instance, for
  - morphology,
  - text to speech,
  - automatic translation,
  - transliteration,
  - spelling correction, ...
- Learning syntax with semantics,
- Unsupervised or semi-supervised learning of linguistic knowledge,
- Learning (classes of) grammars (e.g. subclasses of the Chomsky Hierarchy) from linguistic inputs,
- Comparing learning results in different frameworks (e.g. membership vs. correction queries),
- Learning linguistic structures (e.g. phonological features, lexicon) from the acoustic signal,
- Grammars and finite state machines in machine translation,
- Learning setting of Chomskyan parameters,
- Cognitive aspects of grammar acquisition, covering, among others,
  - developmental trajectories as studied by psycholinguists working with children,
  - characteristics of child-directed speech as they are manifested in corpora such as CHILDES, ...
- (Unsupervised) Computational language acquisition (experimental or observational),

4 The papers

The workshop was glad to have as invited speaker Damir Ćavar, who presented a talk titled: *On bootstrapping of linguistic features for bootstrapping grammars.*

The papers submitted to the workshop and reviewed by at least three reviewers each, covered a very wide range of problems and techniques. Arranging them into patterns was not a simple task!

There were three papers focussing on transducers:

- Jeroen Geertzen shows in his paper *Dialogue Act Prediction Using Stochastic Context-Free Grammar Induction*, how grammar induction can be used in dialogue act prediction.

- In their paper (*Experiments Using OSTIA for a Language Production Task*), Dana Angluin and Leonor Becerra-Bonache build on previous work to see the transducer learning algorithm OSTIA as capable of translating syntax to semantics.

- In their paper titled *GREAT: a finite-state machine translation toolkit implementing a Grammatical Inference Approach for Transducer Inference (GIATI)*, Jorge González and Francisco Casacuberta build on a long history of GOATI learning and try to eliminate some of the limitations of previous work. The learning concerns finite-state transducers from parallel corpora.

Context-free grammars of different types were used for very different tasks:

- Alexander Clark, Remi Eyraud and Amaury Habrard (*A note on contextual binary feature grammars*) propose a formal study of a new formalism called "CBFG", describe the relationship of CBFG to other standard formalisms and its appropriateness for modelling natural language.

- In their work titled *Language models for contextual error detection and correction*, Herman Stehouwer and Menno van Zaanen look at spelling problems as a word prediction problem. The prediction needs a language model which is learnt.

- A formal study of French treebanks is made by Marie-Hélène Candito, Benoit Crabbé and Djamé Seddah in their work: *On statistical parsing of French with supervised and semi-supervised strategies*.

- Franco M. Luque and Gabriel Infante-Lopez study the learnability of NTS grammars with reference to the Penn treebank in their paper titled *Upper Bounds for Unsupervised Parsing with Unambiguous Non-Terminally Separated Grammars*.

One paper concentrated on morphology :

- In *A comparison of several learners for Boolean partitions: implications for morphological paradigm*, Katya Pertsova compares a rote learner to three morphological paradigm learners.

References

P. Adriaans and M. van Zaanen. 2004. Computational grammar induction for linguists. *Grammars*, 7:57–68.

P. Adriaans and M. Vervoort. 2002. The EMILE 4.1 grammar induction toolbox. In Adriaans et al. (Adriaans et al., 2002), pages 293–295.

P. Adriaans, H. Fernau, and M. van Zaannen, editors. 2002. *Grammatical Inference: Algorithms and Applications, Proceedings of* ICGI *'02*, volume 2484 of LNAI, Berlin, Heidelberg. Springer-Verlag.

D. Angluin. 1978. On the complexity of minimum inference of regular sets. *Information and Control*, 39:337–350.

D. Angluin. 1980. Inductive inference of formal languages from positive data. *Information and Control*, 45:117–135.

D. Angluin. 1981. A note on the number of queries needed to identify regular languages. *Information and Control*, 51:76–87.

D. Angluin. 1982. Inference of reversible languages. *Journal of the Association for Computing Machinery*, 29(3):741–765.

D. Angluin. 1987. Queries and concept learning. *Machine Learning Journal*, 2:319–342.

A. Brazma and K. Cerans. 1994. Efficient learning of regular expressions from good examples. In AII *'94: Proceedings of the 4th International Workshop on Analogical and Inductive Inference*, pages 76–90. Springer-Verlag.

A. Brazma, I. Jonassen, J. Vilo, and E. Ukkonen. 1998. Pattern discovery in biosequences. In Honavar and Slutski (Honavar and Slutski, 1998), pages 257–270.

A. Brazma, 1997. *Computational learning theory and natural learning systems*, volume 4, chapter Efficient learning of regular expressions from approximate examples, pages 351–366. MIT Press.

R. C. Carrasco and J. Oncina, editors. 1994. *Grammatical Inference and Applications, Proceedings of* ICGI *'94*, number 862 in LNAI, Berlin, Heidelberg. Springer-Verlag.

N. Chomsky. 1955. *The logical structure of linguistic theory*. Ph.D. thesis, Massachusetts Institute of Technology.

N. Chomsky. 1957. *Syntactic structure*. Mouton.

A. Clark, F. Coste, and L. Miclet, editors. 2008. *Grammatical Inference: Algorithms and Applications, Proceedings of* ICGI *'08*, volume 5278 of LNCS. Springer-Verlag.

C. de la Higuera. 2005. A bibliographical study of grammatical inference. *Pattern Recognition*, 38:1332–1348.

A. L. de Oliveira, editor. 2000. *Grammatical Inference: Algorithms and Applications, Proceedings of* ICGI *'00*, volume 1891 of LNAI, Berlin, Heidelberg. Springer-Verlag.

K. S. Fu and T. L. Booth. 1975. Grammatical inference: Introduction and survey. Part I and II. IEEE *Transactions on Syst. Man. and Cybern.*, 5:59–72 and 409–423.

K. S. Fu. 1974. *Syntactic Methods in Pattern Recognition*. Academic Press, New-York.

E. M. Gold. 1967. Language identification in the limit. *Information and Control*, 10(5):447–474.

E. M. Gold. 1978. Complexity of automaton identification from given data. *Information and Control*, 37:302–320.

J. Goodman. 2001. A bit of progress in language modeling. Technical report, Microsoft Research.

V. Honavar and G. Slutski, editors. 1998. *Grammatical Inference, Proceedings of* ICGI *'98*, number 1433 in LNAI, Berlin, Heidelberg. Springer-Verlag.

J. J. Horning. 1969. *A study of Grammatical Inference*. Ph.D. thesis, Stanford University.

M. Kanazawa. 1998. *Learnable Classes of Categorial Grammars*. CSLI Publications, Stanford, Ca.

M. J. Kearns and U. Vazirani. 1994. *An Introduction to Computational Learning Theory*. MIT press.

L. Miclet and C. de la Higuera, editors. 1996. *Proceedings of* ICGI *'96*, number 1147 in LNAI, Berlin, Heidelberg. Springer-Verlag.

B. L. Natarajan. 1991. *Machine Learning: a Theoretical Approach*. Morgan Kauffman Pub., San Mateo, CA.

G. Paliouras and Y. Sakakibara, editors. 2004. *Grammatical Inference: Algorithms and Applications, Proceedings of* ICGI *'04*, volume 3264 of LNAI, Berlin, Heidelberg. Springer-Verlag.

L. Pitt and M. Warmuth. 1988. Reductions among prediction problems: on the difficulty of predicting automata. In *3rd Conference on Structure in Complexity Theory*, pages 60–69.

L. Pitt and M. Warmuth. 1993. The minimum consistent DFA problem cannot be approximated within any polynomial. *Journal of the Association for Computing Machinery*, 40(1):95–142.

L. Pitt. 1989. Inductive inference, DFA's, and computational complexity. In *Analogical and Inductive Inference*, number 397 in LNAI, pages 18–44. Springer-Verlag, Berlin, Heidelberg.

Y. Sakakibara, S. Kobayashi, K. Sato, T. Nishino, and E. Tomita, editors. 2006. *Grammatical Inference: Algorithms and Applications, Proceedings of* ICGI *'06*, volume 4201 of LNAI, Berlin, Heidelberg. Springer-Verlag.

Y. Sakakibara. 1997. Recent advances of grammatical inference. *Theoretical Computer Science*, 185:15–45.

R. Solomonoff. 1960. A preliminary report on a general theory of inductive inference. Technical Report ZTB-138, Zator Company, Cambridge, Mass.

R. Solomonoff. 1964. A formal theory of inductive inference. *Information and Control*, 7(1):1–22 and 224–254.

M. van Zaanen. 2000. ABL: Alignment-based learning. In *Proceedings of* COLING *2000*, pages 961–967. Morgan Kaufmann.

G. Wolf. 2006. *Unifying computing and cognition*. Cognition research.

On bootstrapping of linguistic features for bootstrapping grammars

Damir Ćavar
University of Zadar
Zadar, Croatia
dcavar@unizd.hr

Abstract

We discuss a cue-based grammar induction approach based on a parallel theory of grammar. Our model is based on the hypotheses of interdependency between linguistic levels (of representation) and inductability of specific structural properties at a particular level, with consequences for the induction of structural properties at other linguistic levels. We present the results of three different cue-learning experiments and settings, covering the induction of phonological, morphological, and syntactic properties, and discuss potential consequences for our general grammar induction model.[1]

1 Introduction

We assume that individual linguistic levels of natural languages differ with respect to their formal complexity. In particular, the assumption is that structural properties of linguistic levels like phonology or morphology can be characterized fully by Regular grammars, and if not, at least a large subset can. Structural properties of natural language syntax on the other hand might be characterized by Mildly context-free grammars (Joshi et al., 1991), where at least a large subset could be characterized by Regular and Context-free grammars.[2]

Ignoring for the time being extra-linguistic conditions and cues for linguistic properties, and independent of the complexity of specific linguistic levels for particular languages, we assume that specific properties at one particular linguistic level correlate with properties at another level. In natural languages certain phonological processes might be triggered at morphological boundaries only, e.g. (Chomsky and Halle, 1968), or prosodic properties correlate with syntactic phrase boundaries and semantic properties, e.g. (Inkelas and Zec, 1990). Similarly, lexical properties, as for example stress patterns and morphological structure tend to be specific to certain word types (e.g. substantives, but not function words). i.e. correlate with the lexical morpho-syntactic properties used in grammars of syntax. Other more informal correlations that are discussed in linguistics, that rather lack a formal model or explanation, are for example the relation between morphological richness and the freedom of word order in syntax.

Thus, it seems that specific regularities and grammatical properties at one linguistic level might provide cues for structural properties at another level. We expect such correlations to be language specific, given that languages qualitatively significantly differ at least at the phonetic, phonological and morphological level, and at least quantitatively also at the syntactic level.

Thus in our model of grammar induction, we favor the view expressed e.g. in (Frank, 2000) that complex grammars are bootstrapped (or grow) from less complex grammars. On the other hand, the intuition that structural or inherent properties at different linguistic levels correlate, i.e. they seem to be used as cues in processing and acquisition, might require a parallel model of language learning or grammar induction, as for example suggested in (Jackendoff, 1996) or the Competition Model (MacWhinney and Bates, 1989).

In general, we start with the observation that

[1]This article is builds on joint work and articles with K. Elghamri, J. Herring, T. Ikuta, P. Rodrigues, G. Schrementi and colleagues at the Institute of Croatian Language and Linguistics and the University of Zadar. The research activities were partially funded by several grants over a couple of years, at Indiana University and from the Croatian Ministry of Science, Education and Sports of the Republic of Croatia.

[2]We are abstracting away from concrete linguistic models and theories, and their particular complexity, as discussed e.g. in (Ristad, 1990) or (Tesar and Smolensky, 2000).

Proceedings of the EACL 2009 Workshop on Computational Linguistic Aspects of Grammatical Inference, pages 5–6,
Athens, Greece, 30 March 2009. ©2009 Association for Computational Linguistics

natural languages are learnable. In principle, the study of how this might be modeled, and what the minimal assumptions about the grammar properties and the induction algorithm could be, could start top-down, by assuming maximal knowledge of the target grammar, and subsequently eliminating elements that are obviously learnable in an unsupervised way, or fall out as side-effects. Alternatively, a bottom-up approach could start with the question about how much supervision has to be added to an unsupervised model in order to converge to a concise grammar.

Here we favor the bottom-up approach, and ask how simple properties of grammar can be learned in an unsupervised way, and how cues could be identified that allow for the induction of higher level properties of the target grammar, or other linguistic levels, by for example favoring some structural hypotheses over others.

In this article we will discuss in detail several experiments of morphological cue induction for lexical classification (Ćavar et al., 2004a) and (Ćavar et al., 2004b) using Vector Space Models for category induction and subsequent rule formation. Furthermore, we discuss structural cohesion measured via Entropy-based statistics on the basis of distributional properties for unsupervised syntactic structure induction (Ćavar et al., 2004c) from raw text, and compare the results with syntactic corpora like the Penn Treebank. We expand these results with recent experiments in the domain of unsupervised induction of phonotactic regularities and phonological structure (Ćavar and Ćavar, 2009), providing cues for morphological structure induction and syntactic phrasing.

References

Damir Ćavar and Małgorzata E. Ćavar. 2009. On the induction of linguistic categories and learning grammars. Paper presented at the 10th Szklarska Poreba Workshop, March.

Damir Ćavar, Joshua Herring, Toshikazu Ikuta, Paul Rodrigues, and Giancarlo Schrementi. 2004a. Alignment based induction of morphology grammar and its role for bootstrapping. In Gerhard Jäger, Paola Monachesi, Gerald Penn, and Shuly Wintner, editors, *Proceedings of Formal Grammar 2004*, pages 47–62, Nancy.

Damir Ćavar, Joshua Herring, Toshikazu Ikuta, Paul Rodrigues, and Giancarlo Schrementi. 2004b. On statistical bootstrapping. In William G. Sakas, editor, *Proceedings of the First Workshop on Psycho-computational Models of Human Language Acquisition*, pages 9–16.

Damir Ćavar, Joshua Herring, Toshikazu Ikuta, Paul Rodrigues, and Giancarlo Schrementi. 2004c. Syntactic parsing using mutual information and relative entropy. Midwest Computational Linguistics Colloquium (MCLC), June.

Noam Chomsky and Morris Halle. 1968. *The Sound Pattern of English*. Harper & Row, New York.

Robert Frank. 2000. From regular to context free to mildly context sensitive tree rewriting systems: The path of child language acquisition. In A. Abeillé and O. Rambow, editors, *Tree Adjoining Grammars: Formalisms, Linguistic Analysis and Processing*, pages 101–120. CSLI Publications.

Sharon Inkelas and Draga Zec. 1990. *The Phonology-Syntax Connection*. University Of Chicago Press, Chicago.

Ray Jackendoff. 1996. *The Architecture of the Language Faculty*. Number 28 in Linguistic Inquiry Monographs. MIT Press, Cambridge, MA.

Aravind Joshi, K. Vijay-Shanker, and David Weird. 1991. The convergence of mildly context-sensitive grammar formalisms. In Peter Sells, Stuart Shieber, and Thomas Wasow, editors, *Foundational Issues in Natural Language Processing*, pages 31–81. MIT Press, Cambridge, MA.

Brian MacWhinney and Elizabeth Bates. 1989. *The Crosslinguistic Study of Sentence Processing*. Cambridge University Press, New York.

Eric S. Ristad. 1990. Computational structure of generative phonology and its relation to language comprehension. In *Proceedings of the 28th annual meeting on Association for Computational Linguistics*, pages 235–242. Association for Computational Linguistics.

Bruce Tesar and Paul Smolensky. 2000. *Learnability in Optimality Theory*. MIT Press, Cambridge, MA.

Dialogue Act Prediction Using Stochastic Context-Free Grammar Induction

Jeroen Geertzen
Research Centre for English & Applied Linguistics
University of Cambridge, UK
jg532@cam.ac.uk

Abstract

This paper presents a model-based approach to dialogue management that is guided by data-driven dialogue act prediction. The statistical prediction is based on stochastic context-free grammars that have been obtained by means of grammatical inference. The prediction performance of the method compares favourably to that of a heuristic baseline and to that of n-gram language models.

The act prediction is explored both for dialogue acts without realised semantic content (consisting only of communicative functions) and for dialogue acts with realised semantic content.

1 Introduction

Dialogue management is the activity of determining how to behave as an interlocutor at a specific moment of time in a conversation: which *action* can or should be taken at what *state* of the dialogue. The systematic way in which an interlocutor chooses among the options for continuing a dialogue is often called a *dialogue strategy*.

Coming up with suitable dialogue management strategies for dialogue systems is not an easy task. Traditional methods typically involve manually crafting and tuning frames or hand-crafted rules, requiring considerable implementation time and cost. More recently, statistical methods are being used to semi-automatically obtain models that can be trained and optimised using dialogue data.[1] These methods are usually based on two assumptions. First, the training data is assumed to be representative of the communication that may be encountered in interaction. Second, it is assumed that dialogue can be modelled as a Markov Decision Process (MDP) (Levin et al., 1998), which implies that dialogue is modelled as a sequential decision task in which each contribution (action) results in a transition from one state to another.

The latter assumption allows to assign a *reward* for action-state pairs, and to determine the dialogue management strategy that results in the maximum expected reward by finding for each state the optimal action by using *reinforcement learning* (cf. (Sutton and Barto, 1998)). Reinforcement learning approaches to dialogue management have proven to be successful in several task domains (see for example (Paek, 2006; Lemon et al., 2006)). In this process there is no supervision, but what is optimal depends usually on factors that require human action, such as task completion or user satisfaction.

The remainder of this paper describes and evaluates a model-based approach to dialogue management in which the decision process of taking a particular action given a dialogue state is guided by data-driven dialogue act prediction. The approach improves over n-gram language models and can be used in isolation or for user simulation, without yet providing a full alternative to reinforcement learning.

2 Using structural properties of task-oriented dialogue

One of the best known regularities that are observed in dialogue are the two-part structures, known as *adjacency pairs* (Schegloff, 1968), like QUESTION-ANSWER or GREETING-GREETING.

A simple model of predicting a plausible next dialogue act that deals with such regularities could be based on bigrams, and to include more context also higher-order n-grams could be used. For instance, Stolcke et al. (2000) explore n-gram models based on transcribed words and prosodic information for SWBD-DAMSL dialogue acts in the Switchboard corpus (Godfrey et al., 1992). After training back-off n-gram models (Katz, 1987) of

[1] See e.g. (Young, 2002) for an overview.

Proceedings of the EACL 2009 Workshop on Computational Linguistic Aspects of Grammatical Inference, pages 7–15,
Athens, Greece, 30 March 2009. ©2009 Association for Computational Linguistics

different order using frequency smoothing (Witten and Bell, 1991), it was concluded that trigrams and higher-order n-grams offer a small gain in predication performance with respect to bigrams.

Apart from adjacency pairs, there is a variety of more complex re-occurring interaction patterns. For instance, the following utterances with corresponding dialogue act types illustrate a clarification sub-dialogue within an information-request dialogue:

1	A: How do I do a fax?	QUESTION
2	B: Do you want to send or print one?	QUESTION
3	A: I want to print it	ANSWER
4	B: Just press the grey button	ANSWER

Such structures have received considerable attention and their models are often referred to as discourse/dialogue grammars (Polanyi and Scha, 1984) or conversational/dialogue games (Levin and Moore, 1988).

As also remarked by Levin (1999), predicting and recognising dialogue games using n-gram models is not really successful. There are various causes for this. The flat horizontal structure of n-grams does not allow (hierarchical) grouping of symbols. This may weaken the predictive power and reduces the power of the representation since nested structures such as exemplified above cannot be represented in a straightforward way.

A better solution would be to express the structure of dialogue games by a context-free grammar (CFG) representation in which the terminals are dialogue acts and the non-terminals denote conversational games. Construction of a CFG would require explicit specification of a discourse grammar, which could be done by hand, but it would be a great advantage if CFGs could automatically be induced from the data. An additional advantage of grammar induction is the possibility to assess the frequency of typical patterns and a stochastic context-free grammar (SCFG) may be produced which can be used for parsing the dialogue data.

3 Sequencing dialogue acts

Both n-gram language models and SCFG based models work on sequences of symbols. Using more complex symbols increases data sparsity: encoding more information increases the number of unique symbols in the dataset and decreases the number of reoccurring patterns which could be used in the prediction.

In compiling the symbols for the prediction experiments, three aspects are important: the identification of interlocutors, the definition of dialogue acts, and multifunctionality in dialogue.

The dialogue act taxonomy that is used in the prediction experiments is that of DIT (Bunt, 2000). A dialogue act is defined as a pair consisting of a communicative function (CF) and a semantic content (SC): $a =< CF, SC >$. The DIT taxonomy distinguishes 11 dimensions of communicative functions, addressing information about the task domain, feedback, turn management, and other generic aspects of dialogue (Bunt, 2006). There are also functions, called *the general-purpose functions*, that may occur in any dimension. In quite some cases, particularly when dialogue control is addressed and dimension-specific functions are realised, the SC is empty. General-purpose functions, by contrast, are always used in combination with a realised SC. For example:

	dialogue act	
utterance	*function*	*semantic content*
What to do next?	SET-QUESTION	`next-step(X)`
Press the button.	SET-ANSWER	`press(Y)` ∧ `button(Y)`

The SC —if realised— describes objects, properties, and events in the domain of conversation.

In dialogue act prediction while taking multidimensionality into account, a dialogue D can be represented as a sequence of events in which an event is a set of one dialogue act or multiple dialogue acts occurring simultaneously. The information concerning interlocutor and multifunctionality is encoded in a single symbol and denoted by means of a n-tuple. Assuming that at most three functions can occur simultaneously, a 4-tuple is needed[2]: `(interlocutor,da1,da2,da3)`. An example of a bigram of 4-tuples would then look as follows:

```
(A,<SET-Q,"next-step(X)">,_,_),
(B,<SET-A,"press(Y) ∧ button(Y)">,_,_)
```

Two symbols are considered to be identical when the same speaker is involved and when the symbols both address the same functions. To make

[2]Ignoring the half percent of occurrences with four simultaneous functions.

it easy to determine if two symbols are identical, the order of elements in a tuple is fixed: functions that occur simultaneously are first ordered on importance of dimension, and subsequently on alphabet. The task-related functions are considered the most important, followed by feedback-related functions, followed by any other remaining functions. This raises the question how recognition performance using multifunctional symbols compares against recognition performance using symbols that only encode the primary function

4 N-gram language models

There exists a significant body of work on the use of language models in relation to dialogue management. Nagata and Morimoto (1994) describe a statistical model of discourse based on trigrams of utterances classified by custom speech act types. They report 39.7% prediction accuracy for the top candidate and 61.7% for the top three candidates.

In the context of the dialogue component of the speech-to-speech translation system VERBMOBIL, Reithinger and Maier (1995) use n-gram dialogue act probabilities to suggest the most likely dialogue act. In later work, Alexandersson and Reithinger (1997) describe an approach which comes close to the work reported in this paper: Using grammar induction, plan operators are semi-automatically derived and combined with a statistical disambiguation component. This system is claimed to have an accuracy score of around 70% on turn management classes.

Another study is that of Poesio and Mikheev (1998), in which prediction based on the previous dialogue act is compared with prediction based on the context of dialogue games. Using the Map Task corpus annotated with 'moves' (dialogue acts) and 'transactions' (games) they showed that by using higher dialogue structures it was possible to perform significantly better than a bigram model approach. Using bigrams, 38.6% accuracy was achieved. Additionally taking game structure into account resulted in 50.6%; adding information about speaker change resulted in an accuracy of 41.8% with bigrams, 54% with game structure.

All studies discussed so far are only concerned with sequences of communicative functions, and disregard the semantic content of dialogue acts.

5 Dialogue grammars

To automatically induce patterns from dialogue data in an unsupervised way, grammatical inference (GI) techniques can be used. GI is a branch of unsupervised machine learning that aims to find structure in symbolic sequential data. In this case, the input of the GI algorithm will be sequences of dialogue acts.

5.1 Dialogue Grammars Inducer

For the induction of structure, a GI algorithm has been implemented that will be referred to as Dialogue Grammars Inducer (DGI). This algorithm is based on distributional clustering and alignment-based learning (van Zaanen and Adriaans, 2001; van Zaanen, 2002; Geertzen and van Zaanen, 2004). Alignment-based learning (ABL) is a symbolic grammar inference framework that has successfully been applied to several unsupervised machine learning tasks in natural language processing. The framework accepts sequences with symbols, aligns them with each other, and compares them to find interchangeable subsequences that mark structure. As a result, the input sequences are augmented with the induced structure.

The DGI algorithm takes as input time series of dialogue acts, and gives as output a set of SCFGs. The algorithm has five phases:

1. SEGMENTATION: In the first phase of DGI, the time series are —if necessary— segmented in smaller sequences based on a specific time interval in which no communication takes place. This is a necessary step in task-oriented conversation in which there is ample time to discuss (and carry out) several related tasks, and an interaction often consists of a series of short dialogues.

2. ALIGNMENT LEARNING: In the second phase a search space of possible structures, called hypotheses, is generated by comparing all input sequences with each other and by clustering sub-sequences that share similar context. To illustrate the alignment learning, consider the following input sequences:

A:SET-Q,	B:PRO-Q,	A:PRO-A,	B:SET-A.
A:SET-Q,	B:PAUSE,	B:RESUME,	B:SET-A.
A:SET-Q,	B:SET-A.		

The alignment learning compares all input sequences with each other, and produces the hypothesised structures depicted below. The induced structure is represented using bracketing.

$[_i$ A:SET-Q, $[_j$ B:PRO-Q, A:PRO-A, $]_j$ B:SET-A. $]_i$
$[_i$ A:SET-Q, $[_j$ B:PAUSE, A:RESUME, $]_j$ B:SET-A. $]_i$
$[_i$ A:SET-Q, $[_j$ $]_j$ B:SET-A. $]_i$

The hypothesis j is generated because of the similar context (which is underlined). The hypothesis i, the full span, is introduced by default, as it might be possible that the sequence is in itself a part of a longer sequence.

3. SELECTION LEARNING: The set of hypotheses that is generated during alignment learning contains hypotheses that are unlikely to be correct. These hypotheses are filtered out, overlapping hypotheses are eliminated to assure that it is possible to extract a context-free grammar, and the remaining hypotheses are selected and remain in the bracketed output. The decision of which hypotheses to select and which to discard is based on a Viterbi beam search (Viterbi, 1967).

4. EXTRACTION: In the fourth phase, SCFG grammars are extracted from the remaining hypotheses by means of recursive descent parsing. Ignoring the stochastic information, a CFG of the above-mentioned example looks in terms of grammar rules as depicted below:

S	⇒	A:SET-Q	**J**	B:SET-A
J	⇒	B:PRO-Q	A:PRO-A	
J	⇒	B:PAUSE	A:RESUME	
J	⇒	$\emptyset$		

5. FILTERING: In the last phase, the SCFG grammars that have small coverage or involve many non-terminals are filtered out, and the remaining SCFG grammars are presented as the output of DGI.

Depending on the mode of working, the DGI algorithm can generate a SCFG covering the complete input or can generate a set of SCFGs. In the former mode, the grammar that is generated can be used for parsing sequences of dialogue acts and by doing so suggests ways to continue the dialogue. In the latter mode, by parsing each grammar in the set of grammars that are expected to represent dialogue games in parallel, specific dialogue games may be recognised, which can in turn be used beneficially in dialogue management.

5.2 A worked example

In testing the algorithm, DGI has been used to infer a set of SCFGs from a development set of 250 utterances of the DIAMOND corpus (see also Section 6.1). Already for this small dataset, DGI produced, using default parameters, 45 'dialogue games'. One of the largest produced structures was the following:

4	**S**	⇒	A:SET-Q , **NTAX** , **NTBT** , B:SET-A
4	**NTAX**	⇒	B:PRO-Q , NTFJ
3	**NTFJ**	⇒	A:PRO-A
1	**NTFJ**	⇒	A:PRO-A , A:CLARIFY
2	**NTBT**	⇒	B:PRO-Q , A:PRO-A
2	**NTBT**	⇒	$\emptyset$

In this figure, each CFG rule has a number indicating how many times the rules has been used. One of the dialogue fragments that was used to induce this structure is the following excerpt:

	utterance	*dialogue act*
A_1	how do I do a short code?	SET-Q
B_1	do you want to program one?	PRO-Q
A_2	no	SET-A
A_3	I want to enter a kie* a short code	CLARIFY
B_2	you want to use a short code?	PRO-Q
A_4	yes	PRO-A
B_3	press the VK button	SET-A

Unfortunately, many of the 45 induced structures were very small or involved generalisations already based on only two input samples. To ensure that the grammars produced by DGI generalise better and are less fragmented, a post-processing step has been added which traverses the grammars and eliminates generalisations based on a low number of samples. In practice, this means that the post-processing requires the remaining grammatical structure to be presented N times or more in the data.[3]. The algorithm without post-processing will be referred to as DGI1; the algorithm with post-processing as DGI2.

6 Act prediction experiments

To determine how to behave as an interlocutor at a specific moment of time in a conversation, the DGI algorithm can be used to infer a SCFG that models the structure of the interaction. The SCFG

[3] $N = 2$ by default, but may increase with the size of the training data.

can then be used to suggest a next dialogue act to continue the dialogue. In this section, the performance of the proposed SCFG based dialogue model is compared with the performance of the well-known n-gram language models, both trained on intentional level, i.e. on sequences of sets of dialogue acts.

6.1 Data

The task-oriented dialogues used in the dialogue act prediction tasks were drawn from the DIAMOND corpus (Geertzen et al., 2004), which contains human-machine and human-human Dutch dialogues that have an assistance seeking nature. The dataset used in the experiments contains $1,214$ utterances representing $1,592$ functional segments from the human-human part of corpus. In the domain of the DIAMOND data, i.e. operating a fax device, the predicates and arguments in the logical expressions of the SC of the dialogue acts refer to entities, properties, events, and tasks in the application domain. The application domain of the fax device is complex but small: the domain model consists of 70 entities with at most 10 properties, 72 higher-level actions or tasks, and 45 different settings.

Representations of semantic content are often expressed in some form of predicate logic type formula. Examples are Quasi Logical Forms (Alshawi, 1990), Dynamic Predicate Logic (Groenendijk and Stokhof, 1991), and Underspecified Discourse Representation Theory (Reyle, 1993). The SC in the dataset is in a simplified first order logic similar to quasi logical forms, and is suitable to support feasible reasoning, for which also theorem provers, model builders, and model checkers can be used. The following utterances and their corresponding SC characterise the dataset:

1	wat moet ik nu doen? *(what do I have to do now?)* λx . next-step(x)
2	druk op een toets *(press a button)* λx . press(x) $\wedge$ button(x)
3	druk op de groene toets *(press the green button)* λx . press(x) $\wedge$ button(x) $\wedge$ color(x,'green')
4	wat zit er boven de starttoets? *(what is located above the starttoets?)* λx . loc-above(x,'button041')

Three types of predicate groups are distinguished: action predicates, element predicates, and property predicates. These types have a fixed order. The action predicates appear before element predicates, which appear in turn before property predicates. This allows to simplify the semantic content for the purpose of reducing data sparsity in act prediction experiments, by stripping away e.g. property predicates. For instance, if desired the SC of utterance 3 in the example could be simplified to that of utterance 2, making the semantics less detailed but still meaningful.

6.2 Methodology and metrics

Evaluation of overall performance in communication is problematic; there are no generally accepted criteria as to what constitutes an objective and sound way of comparative evaluation. An often-used paradigm for dialogue system evaluation is PARADISE (Walker et al., 2000), in which the performance metric is derived as a weighted combination of subjectively rated user satisfaction, task-success measures and dialogue cost. Evaluating if the predicted dialogue acts are considered as positive contributions in such a way would require the model to be embedded in a fully working dialogue system.

To assess whether the models that are learned produce human-like behaviour without resorting to costly user interaction experiments, it is needed to compare their output with real human responses given in the same contexts. This will be done by deriving a model from one part of a dialogue corpus and applying the model on an 'unseen' part of the corpus, comparing the suggested next dialogue act with the observed next dialogue act. To measure the performance, *accuracy* is used, which is defined as the proportion of suggested dialogue acts that match the observed dialogue acts.

In addition to the accuracy, also *perplexity* is used as metric. Perplexity is widely used in relation to speech recognition and language models, and can in this context be understood as a metric that measures the number of equiprobable possible choices that a model faces at a given moment. Perplexity, being related to entropy is defined as follows:

$$Entropy = -\sum_i p(w_i|h) \cdot log_2\, p(w_i|h)$$

$$Perplexity = 2^{Entropy}$$

where h denotes the conditioned part, i.e. w_{i-1} in the case of bigrams and w_{i-2}, w_{i-1} in the case of trigrams, et cetera. In sum, accuracy could be described as a measure of correctness of the hypothesis and perplexity could be described as how probable the correct hypothesis is.

For all n-gram language modelling tasks reported, good-turing smoothing was used (Katz, 1987). To reduce the effect of imbalances in the dialogue data, the results were obtained using 5-fold cross-validation.

To have an idea how the performance of both the n-gram language models and the SCFG models relate to the performance of a simple heuristic, a baseline has been computed which suggests a majority class label according to the interlocutor role in the dialogue. The information seeker has SET-Q and the information provider has SET-A as majority class label.

6.3 Results for communicative functions

The scores for communicative function prediction are presented in Table 1. For each of the three kinds of symbols, accuracy and perplexity are calculated: the first two columns are for the main CF, the second two columns are for the combination of speaker identity *and* main CF, and the third two columns are for the combination of speaker identity and all CFs. The scores for the latter two codings could not be calculated for the 5-gram model, as the data were too sparse.

As was expected, there is an improvement in both accuracy (increasing) and perplexity (decreasing) for increasing n-gram order. After the 4-gram language model, the scores drop again. This could well be the result of insufficient training data, as the more complex symbols could not be predicted well.

Both language models and SCFG models perform better than the baseline, for all three groups. The two SCFG models, DGI1 and DGI2, clearly outperform the n-gram language models with a substantial difference in accuracy. Also the perplexity tends to be lower. Furthermore, model DGI2 performs clearly better than model DGI1, which indicates that the 'flattening' of non-terminals which is described in Section 5 results in better inductions.

When comparing the three groups of sequences, it can be concluded that providing the speaker identity combined with the main communicative function results in better accuracy scores of 5.9% on average, despite the increase in data sparsity. A similar effect has also been reported by Stolcke et al. (2000).

Only for the 5-gram language model, the data become too sparse to learn reliably a language model from. There is again an increase in performance when also the last two positions in the 4-tuple are used and all available dialogue act assignments are available. It should be noted, however, that this increase has less impact than adding the speaker identity. The best performing n-gram language model achieved 66.4% accuracy; the best SCFG model achieved 78.9% accuracy.

6.4 Results for dialogue acts

The scores for prediction of dialogue acts, including SC, are presented in the left part of Table 2. The presentation is similar to Table 1: for each of the three kinds of symbols, accuracy and perplexity were calculated. For dialogue acts that may include semantic content, computing a useful baseline is not obvious. The same baseline as for communicative functions was used, which results in lower scores.

The table shows that the attempts to learn to predict additionally the semantic content of utterances quickly run into data sparsity problems. It turned out to be impossible to make predictions from 4-grams and 5-grams, and for 3-grams the combination of speaker and all dialogue acts could not be computed. Training the SCFGs, by contrast, resulted in fewer problems with data sparsity, as the models abstract quickly.

As with predicting communicative functions, the SCFG models show better performance than the n-gram language models, for which the 2-grams show slightly better results than the 3-grams. Where there was a notable performance difference between DGI1 and DGI2 for CF prediction, for dialogue act prediction there is only a very little difference, which is insignificant considering the relatively high standard deviation. This small difference is explained by the fact that DGI2 becomes less effective as the size of the training data decreases.

As with CF prediction, it can be concluded that providing the speaker identity with the main dialogue act results in better scores, but the difference is less big than observed with CF prediction due to the increased data sparsity.

Table 1: Communicative function prediction scores for n-gram language models and SCFGs in accuracy (*acc*, in percent) and perplexity (*pp*). CF_{main} denotes the main communicative function, SPK speaker identity, and CF_{all} all occurring communicative functions.

	CF_{main}		SPK + CF_{main}		SPK + CF_{all}	
	acc	*pp*	*acc*	*pp*	*acc*	*pp*
baseline	39.1±0.23	24.2±0.19	44.6±0.92	22.0±0.25	42.9±1.33	23.7±0.41
2-gram	53.1±0.88	17.9±0.35	58.3±1.84	16.8±0.31	61.1±1.65	16.3±0.59
3-gram	58.6±0.85	17.1±0.47	63.0±1.98	14.5±0.26	65.9±1.92	14.0±0.23
4-gram	60.9±1.12	16.7±0.15	65.4±1.62	15.2±1.07	66.4±2.03	14.2±0.44
5-gram	60.3±0.43	18.6±0.21	-	-	-	-
DGI1	67.4±3.05	18.3±1.28	74.6±1.94	14.8±1.47	76.5±2.13	13.9±0.35
DGI2	71.8±2.67	16.1±1.25	78.3±2.50	14.0±2.39	78.9±1.98	13.6±0.35

Table 2: Dialogue act prediction scores for n-gram language models and SCFGs. DA_{main} denotes the dialogue act with the main communicative function, and DA_{all} all occurring dialogue acts.

	DA_{main}		SPK + DA_{main}		SPK + DA_{all}			
					full SC		simplified SC	
	acc	*pp*	*acc*	*pp*	*acc*	*pp*	*acc*	*pp*
baseline	18.5±2.01	31.0±1.64	19.3±1.79	27.6±0.93	18.2±1.93	31.6±1.38	18.2±1.93	31.6±1.38
2-gram	31.2±1.42	28.5±1.03	34.6±1.51	24.7±0.62	35.1±1.30	26.9±0.47	37.5±1.34	26.2±2.37
3-gram	29.0±1.14	34.7±2.82	31.9±1.21	30.5±2.06	-	-	29.1±1.28	28.0±2.59
4-gram	-	-	-	-	-	-	-	-
5-gram	-	-	-	-	-	-	-	-
DGI1	38.8±3.27	25.1±0.94	42.5±0.96	25.0±1.14	42.9±2.44	27.3±1.98	46.6±2.01	24.6±2.24
DGI2	39.2±2.45	25.0±1.28	42.7±1.03	25.3±0.99	42.4±2.19	28.0±1.57	46.4±1.94	24.7±2.55

The prediction scores of dialogue acts with full semantic content and simplified semantic content are presented in the right part of Table 2. For both cases multifunctionality is taken into account by including all occurring communicative functions in each symbol. As can be seen from the table, the simplification of the semantic content leads to improvements in the prediction performance for both types of model. The best n-gram language model improved with 2.4% accuracy from 35.1% to 37.5%; the best SCFG-based model improved with 3.7% from 42.9% to 46.6%.

Moreover, the simplification of the semantic content reduced the problem of data-sparsity, making it also possible to predict based on 3-grams although the accuracy is considerably lower than that of the 2-gram model.

7 Discussion

Both n-gram language models and SCFG based models have their strengths and weaknesses. n-gram models have the advantage of being very robust and they can be easily trained. The SCFG based model can capture regularities that have gaps, and allow to model long(er) distance relations. Both algorithms work on sequences and hence are easily susceptible to data-sparsity when the symbols in the sequences get more complex. The SCFG approach, though, has the advantage that symbols can be clustered in the non-terminals of the grammar, which allows more flexibility.

The multidimensional nature of the DIT^{++} functions can be adequately encoded in the symbols of the sequences. Keeping track of the interlocutor and including not only the main communicative function but also other functions that occur simultaneously results in better performance even though it decreases the amount of data to learn from.

The prediction experiments based on main communicative functions assume that in case of multifunctionality, a main function can clearly be identified. Moreover, it is assumed that task-related functions are more important than feedback functions or other functions. For most cases, these assumptions are justified, but in some cases they are problematic. For instance, in a heated discussion, the turn management function could be considered more important for the dialogue than a simultaneously occurring domain specific function. In other cases, it is impossible to clearly identify a main function as all functions occurring simultaneously are equally important to the dialogue.

In general, n-grams of a higher order have a higher predictability and therefore a lower perplexity. However, using high order n-grams is problematic due to sparsity of training data, which clearly is the case with 4-grams, and particularly with 5-grams in combination with complex symbols as for CF prediction.

Considerably more difficult is the prediction of dialogue acts with realised semantic content, as is evidenced in the differences in accuracy and perplexity for all models. Considering that the data set, with about $1,600$ functional segments, is rather small, the statistical prediction of logical expressions increases data sparsity to such a degree that from the n-gram language models, only 2-gram (and 3-grams to some extent) could be trained. The SCFG models can be trained for both CF prediction and dialogue act prediction.

As noted in Section 6.2, objective evaluation of dialogue strategies and behaviour is difficult. The evaluation approach used here compares the suggested next dialogue act with the next dialogue act as observed. This is done for each dialogue act in the test set. This evaluation approach has the advantage that the evaluation metric can easily be understood and computed. The approach, however, is also very strict: in a given dialogue context, continuations with various types of dialogue acts may all be equally appropriate. To also take other possible contributions into account, a rich dataset is required in which interlocutors act differently in similar dialogue context with a similar established common ground. Moreover, such a dataset should contain for each of these cases with similar dialogue context a representative set of samples.

8 Conclusions and future work

An approach to the prediction of communicative functions and dialogue acts has been presented that makes use of grammatical inference to automatically extract structure from corpus data. The algorithm, based on alignment-based learning, has been tested against a baseline and several n-gram language models. From the results it can be concluded that the algorithm outperforms the n-gram models: on the task of predicting the communicative functions, the best performing n-gram model achieved 66.4% accuracy; the best SCFG model achieved 78.9% accuracy. Predicting the semantic content in combination with the communicative functions is difficult, as evidenced by moderate scores. Obtaining lower degree n-gram language models is feasible, whereas higher degree models are not trainable. Prediction works better with the SCFG models, but does not result in convincing scores. As the corpus is small, it is expected that with scaling up the available training data, scores will improve for both tasks.

Future work in this direction can go in several directions. First, the grammar induction approach shows potential of learning dialogue game-like structures unsupervised. The performance on this task could be tested and measured by applying the algorithm on corpus data that have been annotated with dialogue games. Second, the models could also be extended to incorporate more information than dialogue acts alone. This could make comparisons with the performance obtained with reinforcement learning or with Bayesian networks interesting. Third, it would be interesting to learn and apply the same models on other kinds of conversation, such as dialogue with more than two interlocutors. Fourth, datasets could be drawn from a large corpus that covers dialogues on a small but complex domain. This makes it possible to evaluate according to the possible continuations as found in the data for situations with similar dialogue context, rather than to evaluate according to a single possible continuation. Last, the rather unexplored parameter space of the DGI algorithm might be worth exploring in optimising the system's performance.

References

Jan Alexandersson and Norbert Reithinger. 1997. Learning dialogue structures from a corpus. In *Proceedings of Eurospeech 1997*, pages 2231–2234, Rhodes, Greece, September.

Hiyan Alshawi. 1990. Resolving quasi logical forms. *Computational Linguistics*, 16(3):133–144.

Harry Bunt. 2000. Dialogue pragmatics and context specification. In Harry Bunt and William Black, editors, *Abduction, Belief and Context in Dialogue; Studies in Computational Pragmatics*, pages 81–150. John Benjamins, Amsterdam, The Netherlands.

Harry Bunt. 2006. Dimensions in dialogue annotation. In *Proceedings of the 5th International Conference on Language Resources and Evaluation (LREC 2006)*, pages 1444–1449, Genova, Italy, May.

Jeroen Geertzen and Menno M. van Zaanen. 2004. Grammatical inference using suffix trees. In *Proceedings of the 7th International Colloquium on Grammatical Inference (ICGI)*, pages 163–174, Athens, Greece, October.

Jeroen Geertzen, Yann Girard, and Roser Morante. 2004. The DIAMOND project. Poster at the 8th Workshop on the Semantics and Pragmatics of Dialogue (CATALOG 2004), Barcelona, Spain, July.

John Godfrey, Edward Holliman, and Jane McDaniel. 1992. SWITCHBOARD: Telephone speech corpus for research and development. In *Proceedings of the ICASSP-92*, pages 517–520, San Francisco, USA.

Jeroen Groenendijk and Martin Stokhof. 1991. Dynamic predicate logic. *Linguistics and Philosophy*, 14(1):39–100.

Slava M. Katz. 1987. Estimation of probabilities from sparse data for the language model component of a speech recognizer. *IEEE Transactions on Acoustics, Speech, and Signal Processing*, 35(3):400–401.

Oliver Lemon, Kallirroi Georgila, and James Henderson. 2006. Evaluating effectiveness and portability of reinforcement learned dialogue strategies with real users: The talk towninfo evaluation. In *Spoken Language Technology Workshop*, pages 178–181.

Joan A. Levin and Johanna A. Moore. 1988. Dialogue-games: metacommunication structures for natural language interaction. *Distributed Artificial Intelligence*, pages 385–397.

Esther Levin, Roberto Pieraccini, and Wieland Eckert. 1998. Using markov decision process for learning dialogue strategies. In *Proceedings of the ICASSP'98*, pages 201–204, Seattle, WA, USA.

Lori Levin, Klaus Ries, Ann Thymé-Gobbel, and Alon Lavie. 1999. Tagging of speech acts and dialogue games in spanish call home. In *Proceedings of ACL-99 Workshop on Discourse Tagging*, College Park, MD, USA.

Masaaki Nagata and Tsuyoshi Morimoto. 1994. First steps towards statistical modeling of dialogue to predict the speech act type of the next utterance. *Speech Communication*, 15(3-4):193–203.

Tim Paek. 2006. Reinforcement learning for spoken dialogue systems: Comparing strenghts and weaknesses for practical deployment. In *Interspeech Workshop on "Dialogue on Dialogues"*.

Massimo Poesio and Andrei Mikheev. 1998. The predictive power of game structure in dialogue act recognition: Experimental results using maximum entropy estimation. In *Proceedings International Conference on Spoken Language Processing (ICSLP-98)*, Sydney, Australia, December.

Livia Polanyi and Remko Scha. 1984. A syntactic approach to discourse semantics. In *Proceedings of the 10th international conference on Computational linguistics*, pages 413–419, Stanford, CA, USA.

Norbert Reithinger and Elisabeth Maier. 1995. Utilizing statistical dialogue act processing in VERBMOBIL. In *Proceedings of the 33rd annual meeting on the Association for Computational Linguistics (ACL)*, pages 116–121, Cambridge, Massachusetts. Association for Computational Linguistics (ACL).

Uwe Reyle. 1993. Dealing with ambiguities by underspecification: Construction, representation and deduction. *Journal of Semantics*, 10(2):123–179.

Emanuel A. Schegloff. 1968. Sequencing in conversational openings. *American Anthropologist*, 70:1075–1095.

Andreas Stolcke, Klaus Ries, Noah Coccaro, Elizabeth Shriberg, Rebecca Bates, Daniel Jurafsky, Paul Taylor, Rachel Martin, Carol Van Ess-Dykema, and Marie Meteer. 2000. Dialogue act modeling for automatic tagging and recognition of conversational speech. *Computational Linguistics*, 26(3):339–373.

Richard S. Sutton and Andrew G. Barto. 1998. *Reinforcement Learning: An Introduction (Adaptive Computation and Machine Learning)*. MIT Press, March.

Menno van Zaanen and Pieter W. Adriaans. 2001. Comparing two unsupervised grammar induction systems: Alignment-Based Learning vs. EMILE. Technical Report TR2001.05, University of Leeds, Leeds, UK, March.

Menno M. van Zaanen. 2002. *Bootstrapping Structure into Language: Alignment-Based Learning*. Ph.D. thesis, University of Leeds, Leeds, UK, January.

Andrew J. Viterbi. 1967. Error bounds for convolutional codes and an asymptotically optimum decoding algorithm. *IEEE Transactions on Information Theory*, 13(2):260–269, April.

Marilyn Walker, Candace Kamm, and Diane Litman. 2000. Towards developing general models of usability with paradise. *Natural Language Engineering*, 6(3-4):363–377.

Ian H. Witten and Timothy C. Bell. 1991. The zero-frequency problem: Estimating the probabilities of novel events in adaptive text compression. *IEEE Transactions on Information Theory*, 37(4):1085–1094.

Steve Young. 2002. The statistical approach to the design of spoken dialogue systems. Technical Report CUED/F-INFENG/TR.433, Engineering Department, Cambridge University, UK, September.

Experiments Using OSTIA for a Language Production Task

Dana Angluin and **Leonor Becerra-Bonache**
Department of Computer Science, Yale University
P.O.Box 208285, New Haven, CT, USA
{dana.angluin, leonor.becerra-bonache}@yale.edu

Abstract

The phenomenon of meaning-preserving corrections given by an adult to a child involves several aspects: (1) the child produces an incorrect utterance, which the adult nevertheless understands, (2) the adult produces a correct utterance with the same meaning and (3) the child recognizes the adult utterance as having the same meaning as its previous utterance, and takes that as a signal that its previous utterance is not correct according to the adult grammar. An adequate model of this phenomenon must incorporate utterances and meanings, account for how the child and adult can understand each other's meanings, and model how meaning-preserving corrections interact with the child's increasing mastery of language production. In this paper we are concerned with how a learner who has learned to comprehend utterances might go about learning to produce them.

We consider a model of language comprehension and production based on finite sequential and subsequential transducers. Utterances are modeled as finite sequences of words and meanings as finite sequences of predicates. Comprehension is interpreted as a mapping of utterances to meanings and production as a mapping of meanings to utterances. Previous work (Castellanos et al., 1993; Pieraccini et al., 1993) has applied subsequential transducers and the OSTIA algorithm to the problem of learning to comprehend language; here we apply them to the problem of learning to produce language. For ten natural languages and a limited domain of geometric shapes and their properties and relations we define sequential transducers to produce pairs consisting of an utterance in that language and its meaning. Using this data we empirically explore the properties of the OSTIA and DD-OSTIA algorithms for the tasks of learning comprehension and production in this domain, to assess whether they may provide a basis for a model of meaning-preserving corrections.

1 Introduction

The role of corrections in language learning has recently received substantial attention in Grammatical Inference. The kinds of corrections considered are mainly *syntactic corrections* based on proximity between strings. For example, a correction of a string may be given by using edit distance (Becerra-Bonache et al., 2007; Kinber, 2008) or based on the shortest extension of the queried string (Becerra-Bonache et al., 2006), among others. In these approaches semantic information is not used.

However, in natural situations, a child's erroneous utterances are corrected by her parents based on the meaning that the child intends to express; typically, the adult's corrections preserve the intended meaning of the child. Adults use corrections in part as a way of making sure they have understood the child's intentions, in order to keep the conversation "on track". Thus the child's utterance and the adult's correction have the same meaning, but the form is different. As Chouinard and Clark point out (2003), because children attend to contrasts in form, any change in form that does not mark a different meaning will signal to children that they may have produced something that is not acceptable in the target language. Results in (Chouinard and Clark, 2003) show that adults reformulate erroneous child utterances often enough to help learning. Moreover, these re-

Proceedings of the EACL 2009 Workshop on Computational Linguistic Aspects of Grammatical Inference, pages 16–23,
Athens, Greece, 30 March 2009.

sults show that children can not only detect differences between their own utterance and the adult reformulation, but that they do make use of that information.

Thus in some natural situations, corrections have a *semantic* component that has not been taken into account in previous Grammatical Inference studies. Some interesting questions arise: What are the effects of corrections on learning syntax? Can corrections facilitate the language learning process? One of our long-term goals is to find a formal model that gives an account of this kind of correction and in which we can address these questions. Moreover, such a model might allow us to show that semantic information can simplify the problem of learning formal languages.

A simple computational model of *semantics* and *context* for language learning incorporating semantics was proposed in (Angluin and Becerra-Bonache, 2008). This model accommodates two different tasks: comprehension and production. That paper focused only on the comprehension task and formulated the learning problem as follows. The teacher provides to the learner several example pairs consisting of a situation and an utterance denoting something in the situation; the goal of the learner is to learn the meaning function, allowing the learner to comprehend novel utterances. The results in that paper show that under certain assumptions, a simple algorithm can learn to comprehend an adult's utterance in the sense of producing *the same sequence of predicates*, even without mastering the adult's grammar. For example, receiving the utterance *the blue square above the circle*, the learner would be able to produce the sequence of predicates (*bl*, *sq*, *ab*, *ci*).

In this paper we focus on the production task, using sequential and subsequential transducers to model both comprehension and production. Adult production can be modeled as converting a sequence of predicates into an utterance, which can be done with access to the meaning transducer for the adult's language.

However, we do not assume that the child initially has access to the meaning transducer for the adult's language; instead we assume that the child's production progresses through different stages. Initially, child production is modeled as consisting of two different tasks: finding a correct sequence of predicates, and inverting the meaning function to produce a kind of "telegraphic speech". For example, from (*gr*, *tr*, *le*, *sq*) the child may produce *green triangle left square*. Our goal is to model how the learner might move from this telegraphic speech to speech that is grammatical in the adult's sense. Moreover, we would like to find a formal framework in which corrections (in form of expansions, for example, *the green triangle to the left of the square*) can be given to the child during the intermediate stages (before the learner is able to produce grammatically correct utterances) to study their effect on language learning.

We thus propose to model the problem of child language production as a machine translation problem, that is, as the task of translating a sequence of predicate symbols (representing the meaning of an utterance) into a corresponding utterance in a natural language. In this paper we explore the possibility of applying existing automata-theoretic approaches to machine translation to model language production. In Section 2, we describe the use of subsequential transducers for machine translation tasks and review the OSTIA algorithm to learn them (Oncina, 1991). In Section 3, we present our model of how the learner can move from telegraphic to adult speech. In Section 4, we present the results of experiments in the model made using OSTIA. Discussion of these results is presented in Section 5 and ideas for future work are in Section 6.

2 Learning Subsequential Transducers

Subsequential transducers (SSTs) are a formal model of translation widely studied in the literature. SSTs are deterministic finite state models that allow input-output mappings between languages. Each edge of an SST has an associated input symbol and output string. When an input string is accepted, an SST produces an output string that consists of concatenating the output substrings associated with sequence of edges traversed, together with the substring associated with the last state reached by the input string. Several phenomena in natural languages can be easily represented by means of SSTs, for example, the different orders of noun and adjective in Spanish and English (e.g., *un cuadrado rojo - a red square*). Formal and detailed definitions can be found in (Berstel, 1979).

For any SST it is always possible to find an equivalent SST that has the output strings assigned to the edges and states so that they are as close to the initial state as they can be. This is called an Onward Subsequential Transducer (OST).

It has been proved that SSTs are learnable in the limit from a positive presentation of sentence pairs by an efficient algorithm called OSTIA (Onward Subsequential Transducer Inference Algorithm) (Oncina, 1991). OSTIA takes as input a finite training set of input-output pairs of sentences, and produces as output an OST that generalizes the training pairs. The algorithm proceeds as follows (this description is based on (Oncina, 1998)):

- A prefix tree representation of all the input sentences of the training set is built. Empty strings are assigned as output strings to both the internal nodes and the edges of this tree, and every output sentence of the training set is assigned to the corresponding leaf of the tree. The result is called a *tree subsequential transducer*.

- An *onward tree subsequential transducer* equivalent to the tree subsequential transducer is constructed by moving the longest common prefixes of the output strings, level by level, from the leaves of the tree towards the root.

- Starting from the root, all pairs of states of the onward tree subsequential transducer are considered in order, level by level, and are merged if possible (i.e., if the resulting transducer is subsequential and does not contradict any pair in the training set).

SSTs and OSTIA have been successfully applied to different translation tasks: Roman numerals to their decimal representations, numbers written in English to their Spanish spelling (Oncina, 1991) and Spanish sentences describing simple visual scenes to corresponding English and German sentences (Castellanos et al., 1994). They have also been applied to language understanding tasks (Castellanos et al., 1993; Pieraccini et al., 1993).

Moreover, several extensions of OSTIA have been introduced. For example, OSTIA-DR incorporates domain (input) and range (output) models in the learning process, allowing the algorithm to learn SSTs that accept only sentences compatible with the input model and produce only sentences compatible with the output model (Oncina and Varo, 1996). Experiments with a language understanding task gave better results with OSTIA-DR than with OSTIA (Castellanos et al., 1993). Another extension is DD-OSTIA (Oncina, 1998), which instead of considering a lexicographic order to merge states, uses a heuristic order based on a measure of the equivalence of the states. Experiments in (Oncina, 1998) show that better results can be obtained by using DD-OSTIA in certain translation tasks from Spanish to English.

3 From telegraphic to adult speech

To model how the learner can move from telegraphic speech to adult speech, we reduce this problem to a translation problem, in which the learner has to learn a mapping from sequences of predicates to utterances. As we have seen in the previous section, SSTs are an interesting approach to machine translation. Therefore, we explore the possibility of modeling language production using SSTs and OSTIA, to see whether they may provide a good framework to model corrections.

As described in (Angluin and Becerra-Bonache, 2008), after learning the meaning function the learner is able to assign correct meanings to utterances, and therefore, given a situation and an utterance that denotes something in the situation, the learner is able to point correctly to the object denoted by the utterance. To simplify the task we consider, we make two assumptions about the learner at the start of the production phase: (1) the learner's lexicon represents a correct meaning function and (2) the learner can generate correct sequences of predicates.

Therefore, in the initial stage of the production phase, the learner is able to produce a kind of "telegraphic speech" by inverting the lexicon constructed during the comprehension stage. For example, if the sequence of predicates is (*bl*, *sq*, *ler*, *ci*), and in the lexicon *blue* is mapped to *bl*, *square* to *sq*, *right* to *ler* and *circle* to *ci*, then by inverting this mapping, the learner would produce *blue square right circle*.

In order to explore the capability of SSTs and OSTIA to model the next stage of language production (from telegraphic to adult speech), we take the training set to be input-output pairs each of which contains as input a sequence of predicates (e.g., (*bl*, *sq*, *ler*, *ci*)) and as output the corresponding utterance in a natural language (e.g., *the blue square to the right of the circle*). In this example, the learner must learn to include appropriate function words. In other languages, the learner may have to learn a correct choice of words determined by gender, case or other factors. (Note that we are not yet in a position to consider corrections.)

4 Experiments

Our experiments were made for a limited domain of geometric shapes and their properties and relations. This domain is a simplification of the *Miniature Language Acquisition* task proposed by Feldman et al. (Feldman et al., 1990). Previous applications of OSTIA to language understanding and machine translation have also used adaptations and extensions of the Feldman task.

In our experiments, we have predicates for three different shapes (circle (*ci*), square (*sq*) and triangle (*tr*)), three different colors (blue (*bl*), green (*gr*) and red (*re*)) and three different relations (to the left of (*le*), to the right of (*ler*), and above (*ab*)). We consider ten different natural languages: Arabic, English, Greek, Hebrew, Hindi, Hungarian, Mandarin, Russian, Spanish and Turkish.

We created a data sequence of input-output pairs, each consisting of a predicate sequence and a natural language utterance. For example, one pair for Spanish is ((*ci*, *re*, *ler*, *tr*), *el circulo rojo a la derecha del triangulo*). We ran OSTIA on initial segments of the sequence of pairs, of lengths $10, 20, 30, \ldots$, to produce a sequence of subsequential transducers. The whole data sequence was used to test the correctness of the transducers generated during the process. An error is counted whenever given a data pair (x, y), the subsequential transducer translates x to y', and $y' \neq y$. We say that OSTIA has *converged* to a correct transducer if all the transducers produced afterwards have the same number of states and edges, and 0 errors on the whole data sequence.

To generate the sequences of input-output pairs, for each language we constructed a meaning transducer capable of producing the 444 different possible meanings involving one or two objects. We randomly generated 400 unique (non-repeated) input-output pairs for each language. This process was repeated 10 times. In addition, to investigate the effect of the order of presentation of the input-output pairs, we repeated the data generation process for each language, sorting the pairs according to a length-lex ordering of the utterances.

We give some examples to illustrate the transducers produced. Figure 1 shows an example of a transducer produced by OSTIA after just ten pairs of input-output examples for Spanish. This transducer correctly translates the ten predicate sequences used to construct it, but the data is not sufficient for OSTIA to generalize correctly in all cases, and many other correct meanings are still incorrectly translated. For example, the sequence (*ci*, *bl*) is translated as *el circulo a la izquierda del circulo verde azul* instead of *el circulo azul*.

The transducers produced after convergence by OSTIA and DD-OSTIA correctly translate all 444 possible correct meanings. Examples for Spanish are shown in Figure 2 (OSTIA) and Figure 3 (DD-OSTIA). Note that although they correctly translate all 444 correct meanings, the behavior of these two transducers on other (incorrect) predicate sequences is different, for example on (*tr*, *tr*).

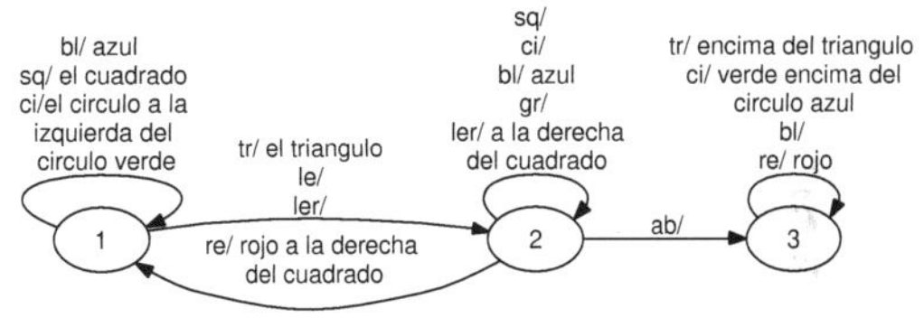

Figure 1: Production task, OSTIA. A transducer produced using 10 random unique input-output pairs (predicate sequence, utterance) for Spanish.

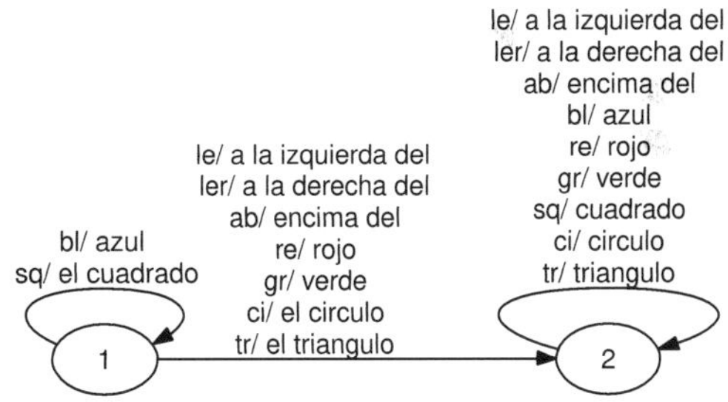

Figure 2: Production task, OSTIA. A transducer produced (after convergence) by using random unique input-output pairs (predicate sequence, utterance) for Spanish.

Different languages required very different numbers of data pairs to converge. Statistics on the number of pairs needed until convergence for OSTIA for all ten languages for both random unique and random unique sorted data sequences are shown in Table 1. Because better results were reported using DD-OSTIA in machine translation

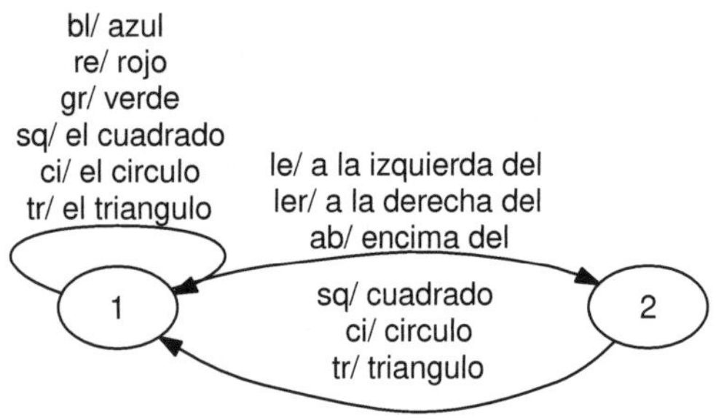

Figure 3: Production task, DD-OSTIA. A transducer produced (after convergence) using random unique input-output pairs (predicate-sequence, utterance) for Spanish.

Language	# Pairs	# Sorted Pairs
Arabic	150	200
English	200	235
Greek	375	400
Hebrew	195	30
Hindi	380	350
Hungarian	365	395
Mandarin	45	150
Russian	270	210
Spanish	190	150
Turkish	185	80

Table 1: Production task, OSTIA. The entries give the median number of input-output pairs until convergence in 10 runs. For Greek, Hindi and Hungarian, the median for the unsorted case is calculated using all 444 random unique pairs, instead of 400.

Language	# Pairs	# Sorted Pairs
Arabic	80	140
English	85	180
Greek	350	400
Hebrew	65	80
Hindi	175	120
Hungarian	245	140
Mandarin	40	150
Russian	185	210
Spanish	80	150
Turkish	50	40

Table 2: Production task, DD-OSTIA. The entries give the median number of input-output pairs until convergence in 10 runs. For Greek, Hindi and Hungarian, the median for the unsorted case is calculated using all 444 random unique pairs, instead of 400.

Languages	#states	#edges
Arabic	2	20
English	2	20
Greek	9	65
Hebrew	2	20
Hindi	7	58
Hungarian	3	20
Mandarin	1	10
Russian	3	30
Spanish	2	20
Turkish	4	31

Table 3: Production task, OSTIA. Sizes of transducers at convergence.

tasks (Oncina, 1998), we also tried using DD-OSTIA for learning to translate a sequence of predicates to an utterance. We used the same sequences of input-output pairs as in the previous experiment. The results obtained are shown in Table 2.

We also report the sizes of the transducers learned by OSTIA and DD-OSTIA. Table 3 and Table 4 show the numbers of states and edges of the transducers after convergence for each language. In case of disagreements, the number reported is the mode.

To answer the question of whether production is harder than comprehension in this setting, we also considered the *comprehension task*, that is, to translate an utterance in a natural language into the corresponding sequence of predicates. The comprehension task was studied by Oncina et al. (Castellanos et al., 1993). They used English sentences, with a more complex version of the Feldman task domain and more complex semantic representations than we use. Our results are presented in Table 5. The number of states and edges of the transducers after convergence is shown in Table 6.

5 Discussion

It should be noted that because the transducers output by OSTIA and DD-OSTIA correctly reproduce all the pairs used to construct them, once either algorithm has seen all 444 possible data pairs in either the production or the comprehension task, the resulting transducers will correctly translate all correct inputs. However, state-merging in the al-

Languages	#states	#edges
Arabic	2	17
English	2	16
Greek	9	45
Hebrew	2	13
Hindi	7	40
Hungarian	3	20
Mandarin	1	10
Russian	3	23
Spanish	2	13
Turkish	3	18

Table 4: Production task, DD-OSTIA. Sizes of transducers at convergence.

Languages	OSTIA	DD-OSTIA
Arabic	65	65
English	60	20
Greek	325	60
Hebrew	90	45
Hindi	60	35
Hungarian	40	45
Mandarin	60	40
Russian	280	55
Spanish	45	30
Turkish	60	35

Table 5: Comprehension task, OSTIA and DD-OSTIA. Median number (in 10 runs) of input-output pairs until convergence using a sequence of 400 random unique pairs of (utterance, predicate sequence).

Languages	#states	#edges
Arabic	1	15
English	1	13
Greek	2	25
Hebrew	1	13
Hindi	1	13
Hungarian	1	14
Mandarin	1	17
Russian	1	24
Spanish	1	14
Turkish	1	13

Table 6: Comprehension task, OSTIA and DD-OSTIA. Sizes of transducers at convergence using 400 random unique input-output pairs (utterance, predicate sequence). In cases of disagreement, the number reported is the mode.

gorithms induces compression and generalization, and the interesting questions are how much data is required to achieve correct generalization, and how that quantity scales with the complexity of the task. This are very difficult questions to approach analytically, but empirical results can offer valuable insights.

Considering the comprehension task (Tables 5 and 6), we see that OSTIA generalizes correctly from at most 15% of all 444 possible pairs except in the cases of Greek, Hebrew and Russian. DD-OSTIA improves the OSTIA results, in some cases dramatically, for all languages except Hungarian. DD-OSTIA achieves correct generalization from at most 15% of all possible pairs for all ten languages. Because the meaning function for all ten language transducers is independent of the state, in each case there is a 1-state sequential transducer that achieves correct translation of correct utterances into predicate sequences. OSTIA and DD-OSTIA converged to 1-state transducers for all languages except Greek, for which they converged to 2-state transducers. Examining one such transducer for Greek, we found that the requirement that the transducer be "onward" necessitated two states. These results are broadly compatible with the results obtained by Oncina et al. (Castellanos et al., 1993) on language understanding; the more complex tasks they consider also give evidence that this approach may scale well for the comprehension task.

Turning to the production task (Tables 1, 2, 3 and 4), we see that providing the random samples with a length-lex ordering of utterances has inconsistent effects for both OSTIA and DD-OSTIA, sometimes dramatically increasing or decreasing the number of samples required. We do not further consider the sorted samples.

Comparing the production task with the comprehension task for OSTIA, the production task generally requires substantially more random unique samples than the comprehension task for the same language. The exceptions are Mandarin (production: 45 and comprehension: 60) and Russian (production: 270 and comprehension: 280). For DD-OSTIA the results are similar, with the sole exception of Mandarin (production: 40 and comprehension: 40). For the production task DD-OSTIA requires fewer (sometimes dramatically fewer) samples to converge than OSTIA. However, even with DD-OSTIA the number of samples is in several cases (Greek, Hindi, Hungarian and Russian) a rather large fraction (40% or more) of all 444 possible pairs. Further experimentation and analysis is required to determine how these results will scale.

Looking at the sizes of the transducers learned by OSTIA and DD-OSTIA in the production task, we see that the numbers of states agree for all languages except Turkish. (Recall from our discussion in Section 4 that there may be differences in the behavior of the transducers learned by OSTIA and DD-OSTIA at convergence.) For the production task, Mandarin gives the smallest transducer; for this fragment of the language, the translation of correct predicate sequences into utterances can be achieved with a 1-state transducer. In contrast, English and Spanish both require 2 states to handle articles correctly. For example, in the transducer in Figure 3, the predicate for a circle (*ci*) is translated as *el circulo* if it occurs as the first object (in state 1) and as *circulo* if it occurs as second object (in state 2) because *del* has been supplied by the translation of the intervening binary relation (*le*, *ler*, or *ab*.) Greek gives the largest transducer for the production task, with 9 states, and requires the largest number of samples for DD-OSTIA to achieve convergence, and one of the largest numbers of samples for OSTIA. Despite the evidence of the extremes of Mandarin and Greek, the relation between the size of the transducer for a language and the number of samples required to converge to it is not monotonic.

In our model, one reason that learning the production task may in general be more difficult than learning the comprehension task is that while the mapping of a word to a predicate does not depend on context, the mapping of a predicate to a word or words does (except in the case of our Mandarin transducer.) As an example, in the comprehension task the Russian words *triugolnik*, *triugolnika* and *triugonikom* are each mapped to the predicate *tr*, but the reverse mapping must be sensitive to the context of the occurrence of *tr*.

These results suggest that OSTIA or DD-OSTIA may be an effective method to learn to translate sequences of predicates into natural language utterances in our domain. However, some of our objectives seem incompatible with the properties of OSTIA. In particular, it is not clear how to incorporate the learner's initial knowledge of the lexicon and ability to produce "telegraphic speech" by inverting the lexicon. Also, the intermediate results of the learning process do not seem to have the properties we expect of a learner who is progressing towards mastery of production. That is, the intermediate transducers perfectly translate the predicate sequences used to construct them, but typically produce other translations that the learner (using the lexicon) would know to be incorrect. For example, the intermediate transducer from Figure 1 translates the predicate sequence (*ci*) as *el circulo a la izquierda del circulo verde*, which the learner's lexicon indicates should be translated as (*ci*, *le*, *ci*, *gr*).

6 Future work

Further experiments and analysis are required to understand how these results will scale with larger domains and languages. In this connection, it may be interesting to try the experiments of (Castellanos et al., 1993) in the reverse (production) direction. Finding a way to incorporate the learner's initial lexicon seems important. Perhaps by incorporating the learner's knowledge of the input domain (the legal sequences of predicates) and using the domain-aware version, OSTIA-D, the intermediate results in the learning process would be more compatible with our modeling objectives. Coping with errors will be necessary; perhaps an explicitly statistical framework for machine translation should be considered.

If we can find an appropriate model of how the learner's language production process might evolve, then we will be in a position to model meaning-preserving corrections. That is, the learner chooses a sequence of predicates and maps it to a (flawed) utterance. Despite its flaws, the learner's utterance is understood by the teacher (i.e., the teacher is able to map it to the sequence of predicates chosen by the learner) and responds with a correction, that is, a correct utterance for that meaning. The learner, recognizing that the teacher's utterance has the same meaning but a different form, then uses the correct utterance (as well as the meaning and the incorrect utterance) to improve the mapping of sequences of predicates to utterances.

It is clear that in this model, corrections are not *necessary* to the process of learning comprehension and production; once the learner has a correct lexicon, the utterances of the teacher can be translated into sequences of predicates, and the pairs of (predicate sequence, utterance) can be used to learn (via an appropriate variant of OSTIA) a perfect production mapping. However, it seems very likely that corrections can make the process of learning a production mapping easier or faster, and finding a model in which such phenomena can be studied remains an important goal of this work.

7 Acknowledgments

The authors sincerely thank Prof. Jose Oncina for the use of his programs for OSTIA and DD-OSTIA, as well as his helpful and generous advice. The research of Leonor Becerra-Bonache was supported by a Marie Curie International Fellowship within the 6th European Community Framework Programme.

References

Dana Angluin and Leonor Becerra-Bonache. 2008. Learning Meaning Before Syntax. *ICGI*, 281–292.

Leonor Becerra-Bonache, Colin de la Higuera, J.C. Janodet, and Frederic Tantini. 2007. Learning Balls of Strings with Correction Queries. *ECML*, 18–29.

Leonor Becerra-Bonache, Adrian H. Dediu, and Cristina Tirnauca. 2006. Learning DFA from Correction and Equivalence Queries. *ICGI*, 281–292.

Jean Berstel. 1979. Transductions and Context-Free Languages. *PhD Thesis*, Teubner, Stuttgart, 1979.

Antonio Castellanos, Enrique Vidal, and Jose Oncina. 1993. Language Understanding and Subsequential Transducers. *ICGI*, 11/1–11/10.

Antonio Castellanos, Ismael Galiano, and Enrique Vidal. 1994. Applications of OSTIA to machine translation tasks. *ICGI*, 93–105.

Michelle M. Chouinard and Eve V. Clark. 2003. Adult Reformulations of Child Errors as Negative Evidence. *Journal of Child Language*, 30:637–669.

Jerome A. Feldman, George Lakoff, Andreas Stolcke, and Susan Hollback Weber. 1990. Miniature Language Acquisition: A touchstone for cognitive science. Technical Report, TR-90-009. International Computer Science Institute, Berkeley, California. April, 1990.

Efim Kinber. 2008. On Learning Regular Expressions and Patterns Via Membership and Correction Queries. *ICGI*, 125–138.

Jose Oncina. 1991. Aprendizaje de lenguajes regulares y transducciones subsecuenciales. *PhD Thesis*, Universitat Politecnica de Valencia, Valencia, Spain, 1998.

Jose Oncina. 1998. The data driven approach applied to the OSTIA algorithm. *ICGI*, 50–56.

Jose Oncina and Miguel Angel Varo. 1996. Using domain information during the learing of a subsequential transducer. *ICGI*, 301–312.

Roberto Pieraccini, Esther Levin, and Enrique Vidal. 1993. Learning how to understand language. *EuroSpeech'93*, 448–458.

GREAT: a finite-state machine translation toolkit implementing a Grammatical Inference Approach for Transducer Inference (GIATI)

Jorge González and **Francisco Casacuberta**
Departamento de Sistemas Informáticos y Computación
Instituto Tecnológico de Informática
Universidad Politécnica de Valencia
{jgonzalez,fcn}@dsic.upv.es

Abstract

GREAT is a finite-state toolkit which is devoted to Machine Translation and that learns structured models from bilingual data. The training procedure is based on grammatical inference techniques to obtain stochastic transducers that model both the structure of the languages and the relationship between them. The inference of grammars from natural language causes the models to become larger when a less restrictive task is involved; even more if a bilingual modelling is being considered. GREAT has been successful to implement the GIATI learning methodology, using different scalability issues to be able to deal with corpora of high volume of data. This is reported with experiments on the EuroParl corpus, which is a state-of-the-art task in Statistical Machine Translation.

1 Introduction

Over the last years, grammatical inference techniques have not been widely employed in the machine translation area. Nevertheless, it is not unknown that researchers are trying to include some structured information into their models in order to capture the grammatical regularities that there are in languages together with their own relationship.

GIATI (Casacuberta, 2000; Casacuberta et al., 2005) is a grammatical inference methodology to infer stochastic transducers in a bilingual modelling approach for statistical machine translation.

From a statistical point of view, the translation problem can be stated as follows: given a source sentence $\mathbf{s} = \mathbf{s}_1 \ldots \mathbf{s}_J$, the goal is to find a target sentence $\hat{\mathbf{t}} = \mathbf{t}_1 \ldots \mathbf{t}_{\hat{I}}$, among all possible target strings $\mathbf{t}$, that maximises the posterior probability:

$$\hat{\mathbf{t}} = \operatorname*{argmax}_{\mathbf{t}} \Pr(\mathbf{t}|\mathbf{s}) \qquad (1)$$

The conditional probability $\Pr(\mathbf{t}|\mathbf{s})$ can be replaced by a joint probability distribution $\Pr(\mathbf{s}, \mathbf{t})$ which is modelled by a stochastic transducer being inferred through the GIATI methodology (Casacuberta et al., 2004; Casacuberta and Vidal, 2004):

$$\hat{\mathbf{t}} = \operatorname*{argmax}_{\mathbf{t}} \Pr(\mathbf{s}, \mathbf{t}) \qquad (2)$$

This paper describes GREAT, a software package for bilingual modelling from parallel corpus.

GREAT is a finite-state toolkit which was born to overcome the computational problems that previous implementations of GIATI (Picó, 2005) had in practice when huge amounts of data were used. Even more, GREAT is the result of a very meticulous study of GIATI models, which improves the treatment of smoothing transitions in decoding time, and that also reduces the required time to translate an input sentence by means of an analysis that will depend on the granularity of the symbols.

Experiments for a state-of-the-art, voluminous translation task, such as the EuroParl, are reported. In (González and Casacuberta, 2007), the so called phrase-based finite-state transducers were concluded to be a better modelling option for this task than the ones that derive from a word-based approach. That is why the experiments here are exclusively related to this particular kind of GIATI-based transducers.

The structure of this work is as follows: first, section 2 is devoted to describe the training procedure, which is in turn divided into several lines, for instance, the finite-state GIATI-based models are defined and their corresponding grammatical inference methods are described, including the techniques to deal with tasks of high volume of data; then, section 3 is related to the decodification process, which includes an improved smoothing behaviour and an analysis algorithm that performs according to the granularity of the bilingual symbols in the models; to continue, section 4 deals

Proceedings of the EACL 2009 Workshop on Computational Linguistic Aspects of Grammatical Inference, pages 24–32,
Athens, Greece, 30 March 2009.

with an exhaustive report on experiments; and finally, the conclusions are stated in the last section.

2 Finite state models

A stochastic finite-state automaton $\mathcal{A}$ is a tuple (Γ, Q, i, f, P), where Γ is an alphabet of symbols, Q is a finite set of states, functions $i : Q \rightarrow [0,1]$ and $f : Q \rightarrow [0,1]$ refer to the probability of each state to be, respectively, initial and final, and parcial function $P : Q \times \{\Gamma \cup \varepsilon\} \times Q \rightarrow [0,1]$ defines a set of transitions between pairs of states in such a way that each transition is labelled with a symbol from Γ (or the empty string ε), and is assigned a probability. Moreover, functions i, f, and P have to respect the *consistency* property in order to define a distribution of probabilities on the free monoid. Consistent probability distributions can be obtained by requiring a series of local constraints which are similar to the ones for stochastic regular grammars (Vidal et al., 2005):

- $\sum_{q \in Q} i(q) = 1$
- $\forall q \in Q : \sum_{\gamma \in \{\Gamma \cup \varepsilon\}, q' \in Q} P(q, \gamma, q') + f(q) = 1$

A stochastic finite-state transducer is defined similarly to a stochastic finite-state automaton, with the difference that transitions between states are labelled with pairs of symbols that belong to two different (input and output) alphabets, that is, $(\Sigma \cup \varepsilon) \times (\Delta \cup \varepsilon)$. Then, given some input and output strings, **s** and **t**, a stochastic finite-state transducer is able to associate them a joint probability $\Pr(\mathbf{s}, \mathbf{t})$. An example of a stochastic finite-state transducer can be observed in Figure 1.

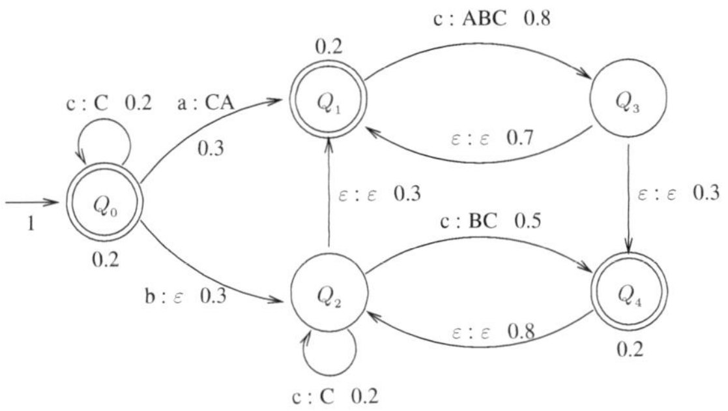

Figure 1: A stochastic finite-state transducer

2.1 Inference of stochastic transducers

The GIATI methodology (Casacuberta et al., 2005) has been revealed as an interesting approach to infer stochastic finite-state transducers through the modelling of languages. Rather than learning translations, GIATI first converts every pair of parallel sentences in the training corpus into a corresponding extended-symbol string in order to, straight afterwards, infer a language model from.

More concretely, given a parallel corpus consisting of a finite sample C of string pairs: first, each training pair $(\bar{x}, \bar{y}) \in \Sigma^\star \times \Delta^\star$ is transformed into a string $\bar{z} \in \Gamma^\star$ from an extended alphabet, yielding a string corpus S; then, a stochastic finite-state automaton $\mathcal{A}$ is inferred from S; finally, transition labels in $\mathcal{A}$ are turned back into pairs of strings of source/target symbols in $\Sigma^\star \times \Delta^\star$, thus converting the automaton $\mathcal{A}$ into a transducer $\mathcal{T}$.

The first transformation is modelled by some labelling function $\mathcal{L} : \Sigma^\star \times \Delta^\star \rightarrow \Gamma^\star$, while the last transformation is defined by an inverse labelling function $\Lambda(\cdot)$, such that $\Lambda(\mathcal{L}(C)) = C$. Building a corpus of extended symbols from the original bilingual corpus allows for the use of many useful algorithms for learning stochastic finite-state automata (or equivalent models) that have been proposed in the literature on grammatical inference.

2.2 Phrase-based n-gram transducers

Phrase-based n-gram transducers represent an interesting application of the GIATI methodology, where the extended symbols are actually bilingual phrase pairs, and n-gram models are employed as language models (González et al., 2008). Figure 2 shows a general scheme for the representation of n-grams through stochastic finite state automata.

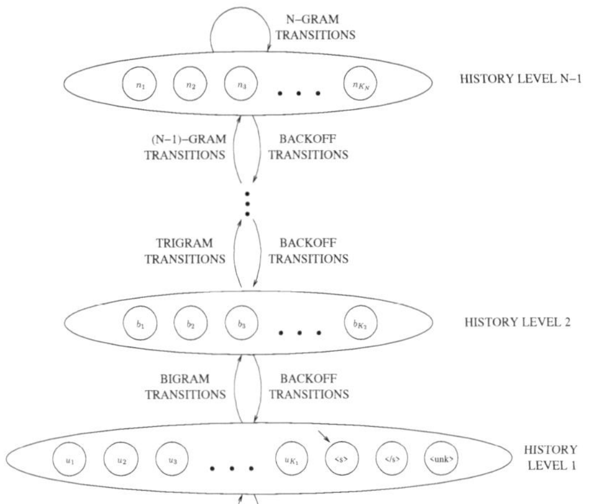

Figure 2: A finite-state n-gram model

The states in the model refer to all the n-gram histories that have been seen in the string corpus S in training time. Consuming transitions jump from states in a determined layer to the one immediately above, increasing the history level. Once the top level has been reached, n-gram transitions allow for movements inside this layer, from state to state, updating the history to the last $n-1$ seen events.

Given that an n-gram event $\Gamma_{n-1}\Gamma_{n-2}\ldots\Gamma_2\Gamma_1\Gamma_0$ is statistically stated as $\Pr(\Gamma_0|\Gamma_{n-1}\Gamma_{n-2}\ldots\Gamma_2\Gamma_1)$, then it is appropriately represented as a finite state transition between their corresponding up-to-date histories, which are associated to some states (see Figure 3).

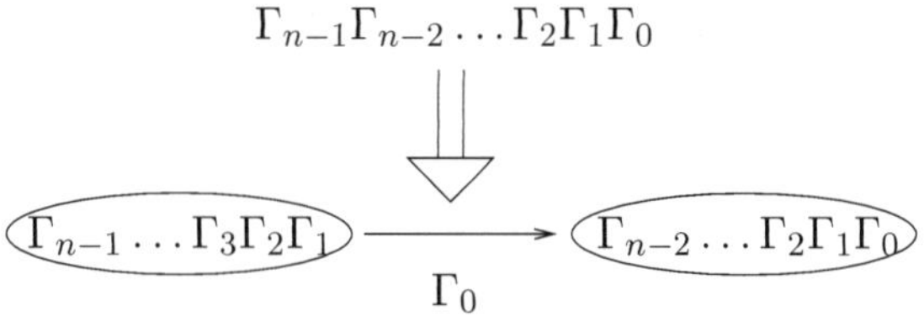

Figure 3: Finite-state representation of n-grams

Therefore, transitions are labelled with a symbol from Γ and every extended symbol in Γ is a translation pair coming from a phrase-based dictionary which is inferred from the parallel corpus.

Nevertheless, backoff transitions to lower history levels are taken for smoothing purposes. If the lowest level is reached and no transition has been found for next word $\mathbf{s}_j$, then a transition to the <unk> state is fired, thus considering $\mathbf{s}_j$ as a non-starting word for any bilingual phrase in the model. There is only 1 initial state, which is denoted as <s>, and it is placed at the 1st history level.

The inverse labelling function is applied over the automaton transitions as in Figure 4, obtaining a single transducer (Casacuberta and Vidal, 2004).

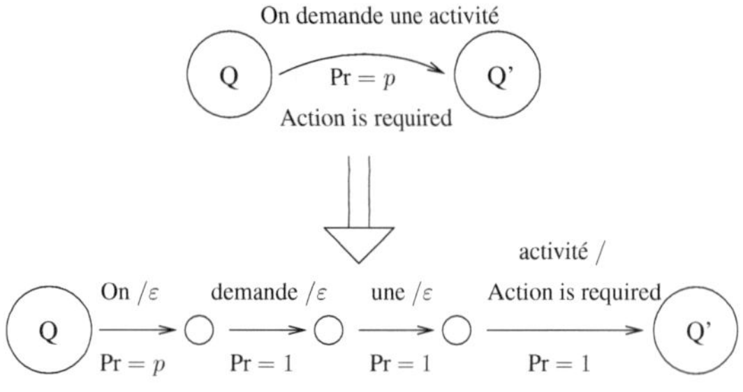

Figure 4: Phrase-based inverse labelling function

Intermediate states are artificially created since they do not belong to the original automaton model. As a result, they are non-final states, with only one incoming and one outcoming edge each.

2.3 Transducer pruning via n-gram events

GREAT implements this pruning technique, which is inspired by some other statistical machine translation decoders that usually filter their phrase-based translation dictionaries by means of the words in the test set sentences (Koehn et al., 2007).

As already seen in Figure 3, any n-gram event is represented as a transition between their corresponding historical states. In order to be able to navigate through this transition, the analysis must have reached the $\Gamma_{n-1}\ldots\Gamma_3\Gamma_2\Gamma_1$ state and the remaining input must fit the source elements of Γ_0. In other words, the full source sequence from the n-gram event $\Gamma_{n-1}\ldots\Gamma_3\Gamma_2\Gamma_1\Gamma_0$ has to be present in the test set. Otherwise, its corresponding transition will not be able to be employed during the analysis of the test set sentences. As a result, n-gram events that are not in the test set can skip their transition generation, since they will not be affected during decoding time, thus reducing the size of the model. If there is also a backoff probability that is associated to the same n-gram event, its corresponding transition generation can be skipped too, since its source state will never be reached, as it is the state which represents the n-gram event. Nevertheless, since trained extended-symbol n-gram events would typically include more than n source words, the verification of their presence or their absence inside the test set would imply hashing all the test-set word sequences, which is rather impractical. Instead, a window size is used to hash the words in the test set, then the trained n-gram events are scanned on their source sequence using this window size to check if they might be skipped or not. It should be clear that the bigger the window size is, the more n-gram rejections there will be, therefore the transducer will be smaller. However, the translation results will not be affected as these disappearing transitions are unreachable using that test set. As the window size increases, the resulting filtered transducer is closer to the minimum transducer that reflects the test set sentences.

3 Finite state decoding

Equation 2 expresses the MT problem in terms of a finite state model that is able to compute the expression $\Pr(\mathbf{s}, \mathbf{t})$. Given that only the input sentence is known, the model has to be parsed, taking into account all possible $\mathbf{t}$ that are compatible with $\mathbf{s}$. The best output hypothesis $\hat{\mathbf{t}}$ would be that one which corresponds to a path through the transduction model that, with the highest probability, accepts the input sequence as part of the input language of the transducer.

Although the navigation through the model is constrained by the input sentence, the search space can be extremely large. As a consequence, only the most scored partial hypotheses are being considered as possible candidates to become the solution. This search process is very efficiently carried out by a beam-search approach of the well known Viterbi algorithm (Jelinek, 1998), whose temporal asymptotic cost is $\Theta(J \cdot |Q| \cdot M)$, where M is the average number of incoming transitions per state.

3.1 Parsing strategies: from words to phrases

The trellis structure that is commonly employed for the analysis of an input sentence through a stochastic finite state transducer has a variable size that depends on the beam factor in a dynamic beam-search strategy. That way, only those nodes scoring at a predefined threshold from the best one in every stage will be considered for the next stage.

A word-based parsing strategy would start with the initial state <s>, looking for the best transitions that are compatible with the first word $\mathbf{s}_1$. The corresponding target states are then placed into the output structure, which will be used for the analysis of the second word $\mathbf{s}_2$. Iteratively, every state in the structure is scanned in order to get the input labels that match the current analysis word $\mathbf{s}_i$, and then to build an output structure with the best scored partial paths. Finally, the states that result from the last analysis step are then rescored by their corresponding final probabilities.

This is the standard algorithm for parsing a source sentence through an non-deterministic stochastic finite state transducer. Nevertheless, it may not be the most appropriate one when dealing with this type of phrase-based n-gram transducers.

As it must be observed in Figure 4, a set of consecutive transitions represent only one phrase translation probability after a given history. In fact, the path from Q to Q' should only be followed if the remaining input sentence, which has not been analysed yet, begins with the full input sequence *On demande une activité*. Otherwise, it should not be taken into account. However, as far as the words in the test sentence are compatible with the corresponding transitions, and according to the phrase score, this (word) synchronous parsing algorithm may store these intermediate states into the trellis structure, even if the full path will not be accomplished in the end. As a consequence, these entries will be using a valuable position inside the trellis structure to an idle result. This will be not only a waste of time, but also a distortion on the best score per stage, reducing the effective power of the beam parameter during the decoding. Some other better analysis options may be rejected because of their a-priori lower score. Therefore, this decoding algorithm can lead the system to a worse translation result. Alternatively, the beam factor can be increased in order to be large enough to store the successful paths, thus more time will be required for the decoding of any input sentence.

On the other hand, a phrase-based analysis strategy would never include intermediate states inside a trellis structure. Instead, these artificial states are tried to be parsed through until an original state is being reached, i.e. Q' in Figure 4. Word-based and phrase-based analysis are conceptually compared in Figure 5, by means of their respective edge generation on the trellis structure.

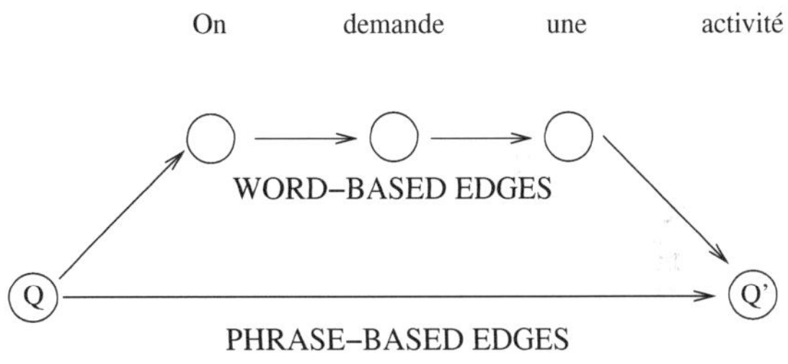

Figure 5: Word-based and phrase-based analysis

However, in order to be able to use a scrolled two-stage implementation of a Viterbi phrase-based analysis, the target states, which may be positioned at several stages of distance from the current one, are directly advanced to the next one. Therefore, the nodes in the trellis must be stored together with their corresponding last input position that was parsed. In the same manner, states in the structure are only scanned if their position indicator is lower than the current analysis word. Otherwise, they have already taken it into account so they are directly transfered to the next stage. The algorithm remains synchronous with the words in the input sentence, however, on this particular occasion, states in the i-th step of analysis are guaranteed to have parsed **at least** until the i-th word, but maybe they have gone further. Figure 6 is a graphical diagram about this concept.

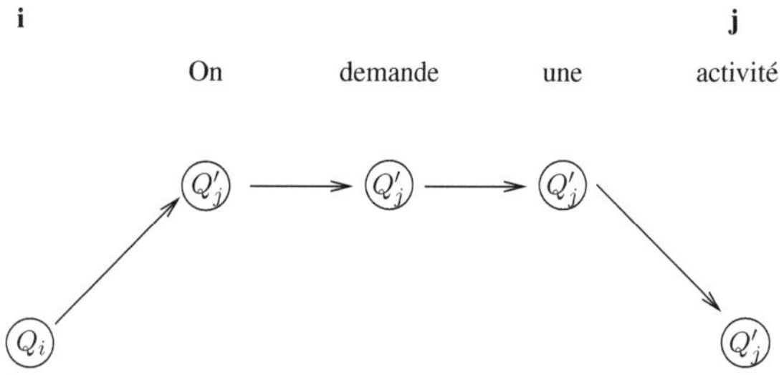

Figure 6: A phrase-based analysis implementation

Moreover, all the states that are being stored in the successive stages, that is, the ones from the original topology of the finite-state representation of the n-gram model, are also guaranteed to lead to a final state in the model, because if they are not final states themselves, then there will always be a successful path towards a final state.

GREAT incorporates an analysis strategy that depends on the granularity of the bilingual symbols themselves so that a phrase-based decoding is applied when a phrase-based transducer is used.

3.2 Backoff smoothing

Two smoothing criteria have been explored in order to parse the input through the GIATI model. First, a standard backoff behaviour, where backoff transitions are taken as failure transitions, was implemented. There, backoff transitions are only followed if there is not any other successful path that has been compatible with the remaining input.

However, GREAT also includes another more refined smoothing behaviour, to be applied over the same bilingual n-gram transducers, where smoothing edges are interpreted in a different way.

GREAT suggests to apply the backoff criterion according to its definition in the grammatical inference method which incorporated it into the language model being learnt and that will be represented as a stochastic finite-state automaton. In other words, from the n-gram point of view, backoff weights (or finite-state transitions) should only be employed if no transitions are found in the n-gram automaton for a current **bilingual** symbol. Nevertheless, input words in translation applications do not belong to those bilingual languages. Instead, input sequences have to be analysed in such a way as if they could be internally representing any possible bilingual symbol from the extended vocabulary that matches their source sides. That way, bilingual symbols are considered to be a sort of input, so the backoff smoothing criterion is then applied to each compatible, bilingual symbol.

For phrase-based transducers, it means that for a successful transition $(\bar{x}, \bar{y})$, there is no need to go backoff and find other paths consuming that bilingual symbol, but we must try backoff transitions to look for any other successful transition $(\bar{x}', \bar{y}')$, which is also compatible with the current position.

Conceptually, this procedure would be as if the input sentence, rather than a source string, was actually composed of a left-to-right bilingual graph, being built from the expansion of every input word into their compatible, bilingual symbols as in a category-based approach. Phrase-based bilingual symbols would be graphically represented as a sort of skip transitions inside this bilingual input graph.

This new interpretation about the backoff smoothing weights on bilingual n-gram models, which is not a priori a trivial feature to be included, is easily implemented for stochastic transducers by considering backoff transitions as ε/ε transitions and keeping track of a dynamic list of forbidden states every time a backoff transition is taken.

An outline about the management of state activeness, which is integrated into the parsing algorithm, is shown below:

ALGORITHM

```
for Q in {states to explore}
  for Q-Q' in {transitions}   (a)
    if Q' is active
      [...]
      set Q' to inactive
  if Q is not NULL
    if Q not in the top level
      for Q' in {inactive states}
        set Q'  to active
        Q'' := backoff(Q')
        set Q'' to inactive
    Q := backoff(Q)
    GoTo (a)
  else
    [...]
    for Q' in {inactive states}
      set Q' to active
[...]
```

END ALGORITHM

The algorithm will try to translate several consecutive input words as a whole phrase, always allowing a backoff transition in order to cover all the compatible phrases in the model, not only the ones which have been seen after a given history, but after all its suffixes as well. A dynamic list of forbidden states will take care to accomplish an exploration constraint that has to be included into the parsing algorithm: a path between two states Q and Q' has necessarily to be traced through the minimum number of backoff transitions; any other Q-Q' or Q-Q" paths, where Q" is the destination of a Q'-Q" backoff path, should be ignored. This constraint will cause that only one transition per bilingual symbol will be followed, and that it will be the highest in the hierarchy of history levels. Figure 7 shows a parsing example over a finite-state representation of a smoothed bigram model.

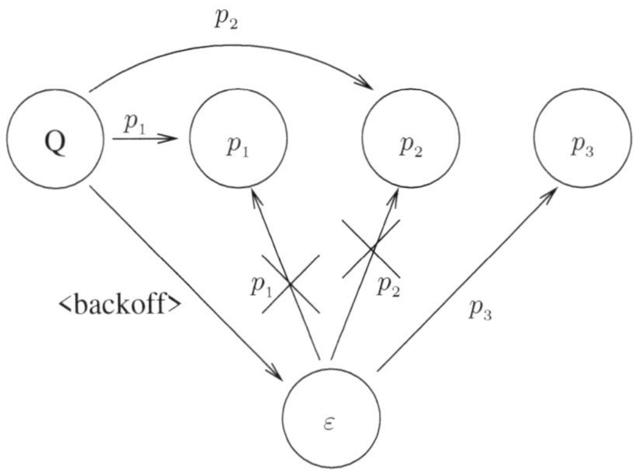

Figure 7: *Compatible edges for a bigram model.* Given a reaching state Q, let us assume that the transitions that correspond to certain bilingual phrase pairs p_1, p_2 and p_3 are all compatible with the remaining input. However, the bigram (Q, p_3) did not occur throughout the training corpus, therefore there is no a direct transition from Q to p_3. A backoff transition enables the access to p_3 because the bigram (Q, p_3) turns into a unigram event that is actually inside the model. Unigram transitions to p_1 and p_2 must be ignored because their corresponding bigram events were successfully found one level above.

4 Experiments

GREAT has been successfully employed to work with the French-English EuroParl corpus, that is, the benchmark corpus of the NAACL 2006 shared task of the Workshop on Machine Translation of the Association for Computational Linguistics. The corpus characteristics can be seen in Table 1.

Table 1: *Characteristics of the Fr-En EuroParl.*

		French	**English**
Training	Sentences	688031	
	Run. words	15.6 M	13.8 M
	Vocabulary	80348	61626
Dev-Test	Sentences	2000	
	Run. words	66200	57951

The EuroParl corpus is built on the proceedings of the European Parliament, which are published on its web and are freely available. Because of its nature, this corpus has a large variability and complexity, since the translations into the different official languages are performed by groups of human translators. The fact that not all translators agree in their translation criteria implies that a given source sentence can be translated in various different ways throughout the corpus.

Since the proceedings are not available in every language as a whole, a different subset of the corpus is extracted for every different language pair, thus evolving into somewhat a different corpus for each pair of languages.

4.1 System evaluation

We evaluated the performance of our methods by using the following evaluation measures:

BLEU *(Bilingual Evaluation Understudy) score*: This indicator computes the precision of unigrams, bigrams, trigrams, and tetragrams with respect to a set of reference translations, with a penalty for too short sentences (Papineni et al., 2001). BLEU measures accuracy, not error rate.

WER *(Word Error Rate)*: The WER criterion calculates the minimum number of editions (substitutions, insertions or deletions) that are needed to convert the system hypothesis into the sentence considered ground truth. Because of its nature, this measure is very pessimistic.

Time. It refers to the average time (in milliseconds) to translate one word from the test corpus, without considering loading times.

4.2 Results

A set of experimental results were obtained in order to assess the impact of the proposed techniques in the work with phrase-based n-gram transducers.

By assuming an unconstrained parsing, that is, the successive trellis structure is large enough to store all the states that are compatible within the analysis of a source sentence, the results are not very sensitive to the n-gram degree, just showing that bigrams are powerful enough for this corpus. However, apart from this, Table 2 is also showing a significant better performance for the second, more refined behaviour for the backoff transitions.

Table 2: *Results for the two smoothing criteria.*

Backoff	n = 1	2	3	4	5
baseline					
BLEU	26.8	26.3	25.8	25.7	25.7
WER	62.3	63.9	64.5	64.5	64.5
GREAT					
BLEU	26.8	**28.0**	27.9	27.9	27.9
WER	62.3	**61.9**	62.0	62.0	62.0

From now on, the algorithms will be tested on the phrase-based *bigram* transducer, being built according to the GIATI method, where backoff is employed as ε/ε transitions with forbidden states.

In these conditions, the results, following a word-based and a phrase-based decoding strategy, which are in function of the dynamic beam factor, can be analysed in Tables 3 and 4.

Table 3: *Results for a word-based analysis.*

beam	Time (ms)	BLEU	WER
1.00	0.1	0.4	94.6
1.02	0.3	12.8	81.9
1.05	5.2	20.0	74.0
1.10	30.0	24.9	68.2
1.25	99.0	27.1	64.6
1.50	147.0	27.5	62.9
2.00	173.6	27.8	62.1
3.50	252.3	28.0	61.9

From the comparison of Tables 3 and 4, it can be deduced that a word-based analysis is iteratively taking into account a quite high percentage of useless states, thus needing to increase the beam parameter to include the successful paths into the analysis. The price for considering such a long list of states in every iteration of the algorithm is in terms of temporal requirements.

Table 4: *Results for a phrase-based analysis.*

beam	Time (ms)	BLEU	WER
1.00	0.2	19.8	71.8
1.02	0.4	22.1	68.6
1.05	0.7	24.3	66.0
1.10	2.4	26.1	64.2
1.25	7.0	27.1	62.8
1.50	9.7	27.5	62.3
2.00	11.4	27.8	62.0
3.50	**12.3**	28.0	61.9

However, a phrase-based approach only stores those states that have been successfully reached by a full phrase compatibility with the input sentence. Therefore, it takes more time to process an individual state, but since the list of states is shorter, the search method performs at a better speed rate. Another important element to point out between Tables 3 and 4, is about the differences on quality results for a same beam parameter in both tables. Word-based decoding strategies suffer the effective reduction on the beam factor that was mentioned on section 3.1 because their best scores on every analysis stage, which determine the exploration boundaries, may refer to a no way out path. Logically, these differences are progressively reduced as the beam parameter increases, since the search space is explored in a more exhaustive way.

Table 5: *Number of trained and survived n-grams.*

Window size	n-grams: unigrams	bigrams
No filter	1,593,677	4,477,382
2	299,002	512,943
3	153,153	141,883
4	130,666	90,265
5	126,056	78,824
6	125,516	77,341

On the other hand, a phrase-based extended-symbol bigram model, being learnt by means of the full training data, computes an overall set of approximately 6 million events. The application of the n-gram pruning technique, using a growing window parameter, can effectively reduce that number to only 200,000. These n-grams, when represented as transducer transitions, suppose a reduction from 20 million transitions to only those

500,000 that are affected by the test set sentences. As a result, the size of the model to be parsed decreases, therefore, the decoding time also decreases. Tables 5 and 6 show the effect of this pruning method on the size of the transducers, then on the decoding time with a phrase-based analysis, which is the best strategy for phrase-based models.

Table 6: *Decoding time for several windows sizes.*

Window size	Edges	Time (ms)
No filter	19,333,520	362.4
2	2,752,882	41.3
3	911,054	17.3
4	612,006	12.8
5	541,059	11.9
6	531,333	11.8

Needless to say that BLEU and WER keep on their best numbers for all the transducer sizes as the test set is not present in the pruned transitions.

5 Conclusions

GIATI is a grammatical inference technique to learn stochastic transducers from bilingual data for their usage in statistical machine translation. Finite-state transducers are able to model both the structure of both languages and their relationship. GREAT is a finite-state toolkit which was born to overcome the computational problems that previous implementations of GIATI present in practice when huge amounts of parallel data are employed.

Moreover, GREAT is the result of a very meticulous study of GIATI models, which improves the treatment of smoothing transitions in decoding time, and that also reduces the required time to translate an input sentence by means of an analysis that will depend on the granularity of the symbols.

A pruning technique has been designed for n-gram approaches, which reduces the transducer size to integrate only those transitions that are really required for the translation of the test set. That has allowed us to perform some experiments concerning a state-of-the-art, voluminous translation task, such as the EuroParl, whose results have been reported in depth. A better performance has been found when a phrase-based decoding strategy is selected in order to deal with those GIATI phrase-based transducers. Besides, this permits us to apply a more refined interpretation of backoff transitions for a better smoothing translation behaviour.

Acknowledgments

This work was supported by the "Vicerrectorado de Innovación y Desarrollo de la Universidad Politécnica de Valencia", under grant 20080033.

References

Francisco Casacuberta and Enrique Vidal. 2004. Machine translation with inferred stochastic finite-state transducers. *Comput. Linguistics*, 30(2):205–225.

Francisco Casacuberta, Hermann Ney, Franz Josef Och, Enrique Vidal, Juan Miguel Vilar, Sergio Barrachina, Ismael García-Varea, David Llorens, César Martínez, and Sirko Molau. 2004. Some approaches to statistical and finite-state speech-to-speech translation. *Computer Speech & Language*, 18(1):25–47.

Francisco Casacuberta, Enrique Vidal, and David Picó. 2005. Inference of finite-state transducers from regular languages. *Pattern Recognition*, 38(9):1431–1443.

F. Casacuberta. 2000. Inference of finite-state transducers by using regular grammars and morphisms. In A.L. Oliveira, editor, *Grammatical Inference: Algorithms and Applications*, volume 1891 of *Lecture Notes in Computer Science*, pages 1–14. Springer-Verlag. 5th International Colloquium Grammatical Inference -ICGI2000-. Lisboa. Portugal.

J. González and F. Casacuberta. 2007. Phrase-based finite state models. In *Proceedings of the 6th International Workshop on Finite State Methods and Natural Language Processing (FSMNLP)*, Potsdam (Germany), September 14-16.

J. González, G. Sanchis, and F. Casacuberta. 2008. Learning finite state transducers using bilingual phrases. In *9th International Conference on Intelligent Text Processing and Computational Linguistics. Lecture Notes in Computer Science*, Haifa, Israel, February 17 to 23.

Frederick Jelinek. 1998. *Statistical Methods for Speech Recognition*. The MIT Press, January.

Philipp Koehn, Hieu Hoang, Alexandra Birch, Chris Callison-Burch, Marcello Federico, Nicola Bertoldi, Brooke Cowan, Wade Shen, Christine Moran, Richard Zens, Chris Dyer, Ondrej Bojar, Alexandra Constantin, and Evan Herbst. 2007. Moses: Open source toolkit for statistical machine translation. In *ACL*. The Association for Computer Linguistics.

K. Papineni, S. Roukos, T. Ward, and W. Zhu. 2001. Bleu: a method for automatic evaluation of machine translation.

David Picó. 2005. *Combining Statistical and Finite-State Methods for Machine Translation*. Ph.D. thesis, Departamento de Sistemas Informáticos y Computación. Universidad Politécnica de Valencia, Valencia (Spain), September. Advisor: Dr. F. Casacuberta.

E. Vidal, F. Thollard, F. Casacuberta C. de la Higuera, and R. Carrasco. 2005. Probabilistic finite-state machines - part I. *IEEE Transactions on Pattern Analysis and Machine Intelligence*, 27(7):1013–1025.

A note on contextual binary feature grammars

Alexander Clark
Department of Computer Science
Royal Holloway, University of London
alexc@cs.rhul.ac.uk

Rémi Eyraud and **Amaury Habrard**
Laboratoire d'Informatique Fondamentale
de Marseille, CNRS,
Aix-Marseille Université, France
remi.eyraud,amaury.habrard@lif.univ-mrs.fr

Abstract

Contextual Binary Feature Grammars were recently proposed by (Clark et al., 2008) as a learnable representation for richly structured context-free and context sensitive languages. In this paper we examine the representational power of the formalism, its relationship to other standard formalisms and language classes, and its appropriateness for modelling natural language.

1 Introduction

An important issue that concerns both natural language processing and machine learning is the ability to learn suitable structures of a language from a finite sample. There are two major points that have to be taken into account in order to define a learning method useful for the two fields: first the method should rely on intrinsic properties of the language itself, rather than syntactic properties of the representation. Secondly, it must be possible to associate some semantics to the structural elements in a natural way.

Grammatical inference is clearly an important technology for NLP as it will provide a foundation for theoretically well-founded unsupervised learning of syntax, and thus avoid the annotation bottleneck and the limitations of working with small hand-labelled treebanks.

Recent advances in context-free grammatical inference have established that there are large learnable classes of context-free languages. In this paper, we focus on the basic representation used by the recent approach proposed in (Clark et al., 2008). The authors consider a formalism called *Contextual Binary Feature Grammars (CBFG)* which defines a class of grammars using contexts as features instead of classical non terminals. The use of features is interesting from an NLP point of view because we can associate some semantics to them, and because we can represent complex, structured syntactic categories. The notion of contexts is relevant from a grammatical inference standpoint since they are easily observable from a finite sample. In this paper we establish some basic language theoretic results about the class of exact Contextual Binary Feature Grammars (defined in Section 3), in particular their relationship to the Chomsky hierarchy: exact CBFGs are those where the contextual features are associated to all the possible strings that can appear in the corresponding contexts of the language defined by the grammar.

The main results of this paper are proofs that the class of exact CBFGs:

- properly includes the regular languages (Section 5),
- does not include some context-free languages (Section 6),
- and does include some non context-free languages (Section 7).

Thus, this class of exact CBFGs is orthogonal to the classic Chomsky hierarchy but can represent a very large class of languages. Moreover, it has been shown that this class is efficiently learnable. This class is therefore an interesting candidate for modeling natural language and deserves further investigation.

2 Basic Notation

We consider a finite alphabet Σ, and Σ^* the free monoid generated by Σ. λ is the empty string, and a language is a subset of Σ^*. We will write the concatenation of u and v as uv, and similarly for sets of strings. $u \in \Sigma^*$ is a substring of $v \in \Sigma^*$ if there are strings $l, r \in \Sigma^*$ such that $v = lur$.

Proceedings of the EACL 2009 Workshop on Computational Linguistic Aspects of Grammatical Inference, pages 33–40,
Athens, Greece, 30 March 2009. ©2009 Association for Computational Linguistics

A context is an element of $\Sigma^* \times \Sigma^*$. For a string u and a context $f = (l, r)$ we write $f \odot u = lur$; the insertion or wrapping operation. We extend this to sets of strings and contexts in the natural way. A context is also known in structuralist linguistics as an *environment*.

The set of contexts, or *distribution*, of a string u of a language L is, $C_L(u) = \{(l, r) \in \Sigma^* \times \Sigma^* | lur \in L\}$. We will often drop the subscript where there is no ambiguity. We define the *syntactic congruence* as $u \equiv_L v$ iff $C_L(u) = C_L(v)$. The equivalence classes under this relation are the *congruence* classes of the language. In general we will assume that λ is not a member of any language.

3 Contextual Binary Feature Grammars

Most definitions and lemmas of this section were first introduced in (Clark et al., 2008).

3.1 Definition

Before the presentation of the formalism, we give some results about contexts to help to give an intuition of the representation. The basic insight behind CBFGs is that there is a relation between the contexts of a string w and the contexts of its substrings. This is given by the following trivial lemma:

Lemma 1. *For any language L and for any strings u, u', v, v' if $C(u) = C(u')$ and $C(v) = C(v')$, then $C(uv) = C(u'v')$.*

We can also consider a slightly stronger result:

Lemma 2. *For any language L and for any strings u, u', v, v' if $C(u) \subseteq C(u')$ and $C(v) \subseteq C(v')$, then $C(uv) \subseteq C(u'v')$.*

$C(u) \subseteq C(u')$ means that we can replace any occurrence of u in a sentence, with a u', without affecting the grammaticality, but not necessarily vice versa. Note that none of these strings need to correspond to non-terminals: this is valid for any fragment of a sentence.

We will give a simplified example from English syntax: the pronoun *it* can occur everywhere that the pronoun *him* can, but not vice versa[1]. Thus given a sentence "I gave him away", we can substitute *it* for *him*, to get the grammatical sentence *I gave it away*, but we cannot reverse the process. For example, given the sentence *it is raining*, we cannot substitute *him* for *it*, as we will get the ungrammatical sentence *him is raining*. Thus we observe $C(him) \subsetneq C(it)$.

Looking at Lemma 2 we can also say that, if we have some finite set of strings K, where we know the contexts, then:

Corollary 1.

$$C(w) \supseteq \bigcup_{\substack{u',v':\\ u'v'=w}} \; \bigcup_{\substack{u \in K:\\ C(u) \subseteq C(u')}} \; \bigcup_{\substack{v \in K:\\ C(v) \subseteq C(v')}} C(uv)$$

This is the basis of the representation: a word w is characterised by its set of contexts. We can compute the representation of w, from the representation of its parts u', v', by looking at all of the other matching strings u and v where we understand how they combine (with subset inclusion). In order to illustrate this concept, we give here a simple example.

Consider the language $\{a^n b^n | n > 0\}$ and the set $K = \{aabb, ab, abb, aab, a, b\}$. Suppose we want to compute the set of contexts of $aaabbb$, Since $C(abb) \subseteq C(aabbb)$, and vacuously $C(a) \subseteq C(a)$, we know that $C(aabb) \subseteq C(aaabbb)$. More generally, the contexts of ab can represent $a^n b^n$, those of aab the strings $a^{n+1} b^n$ and the ones of abb the strings $a^n b^{n+1}$.

The key relationships are given by context set inclusion. *Contextual binary feature grammars* allow a proper definition of the combination of context inclusion:

Definition 1. *A Contextual Binary Feature Grammar (CBFG) G is a tuple $\langle F, P, P_L, \Sigma \rangle$. F is a finite set of contexts, called features, where we write $C = 2^F$ for the power set of F defining the categories of the grammar, $P \subseteq C \times C \times C$ is a finite set of productions that we write $x \rightarrow yz$ where $x, y, z \in C$ and $P_L \subseteq C \times \Sigma$ is a set of lexical rules, written $x \rightarrow a$.*

Normally P_L contains exactly one production for each letter in the alphabet (the lexicon).

A CBFG G defines recursively a map f_G

[1] This example does not account for a number of syntactic and semantic phenomena, particularly the distribution of reflexive anaphors.

from $\Sigma^* \to C$ as follows:

$$f_G(\lambda) = \emptyset \quad (1)$$

$$f_G(w) = \bigcup_{(c \to w) \in P_L} c \qquad \text{iff } |w| = 1 \quad (2)$$

$$f_G(w) = \bigcup_{u,v: uv=w} \bigcup_{\substack{x \to yz \in P: \\ y \subseteq f_G(u) \wedge \\ z \subseteq f_G(v)}} x \qquad \text{iff } |w| > 1. \quad (3)$$

We give here more explanation about the map f_G. It defines in fact the analysis of a string by a CBFG. A rule $z \to xy$ is applied to analyse a string w if there is a cut $uv = w$ s.t. $x \subseteq f_G(u)$ and $y \subseteq f_G(v)$, recall that x and y are sets of contexts. Intuitively, the relation given by the production rule is linked with Lemma 2: z is included in the set of features of $w = uv$. From this relationship, for any $(l, r) \in z$ we have $lwr \in L(G)$.

The complete computation of f_G is then justified by Corollary 1: $f_G(w)$ defines all the possible features associated by G to w with all the possible cuts $uv = w$ (*i.e.* all the possible derivations).

Finally, the natural way to define the membership of a string w in $L(G)$ is to have the context $(\lambda, \lambda) \in f_G(w)$ which implies that $\lambda u \lambda = u \in L(G)$.

Definition 2. *The language defined by a CBFG G is the set of all strings that are assigned the empty context:* $L(G) = \{u | (\lambda, \lambda) \in f_G(u)\}$.

As we saw before, we are interested in cases where there is a correspondence between the language theoretic interpretation of a context, and the occurrence of that context as a feature in the grammar. From the basic definition of a CBFG, we do not require any specific condition on the features of the grammar, except that a feature is associated to a string if the string appears in the context defined by the feature. However, we can also require that f_G defines exactly all the possible features that can be associated to a given string according to the underlying language.

Definition 3. *Given a finite set of contexts* $F = \{(l_1, r_1), \ldots, (l_n, r_n)\}$ *and a language L we can define the context feature map* $F_L : \Sigma^* \to 2^F$ *which is just the map* $u \mapsto \{(l, r) \in F | lur \in L\} = C_L(u) \cap F$.

Using this definition, we now need a correspondence between the language theoretic context feature map F_L and the representation in the CBFG f_G.

Definition 4. *A CBFG G is* exact *if for all* $u \in \Sigma^*$, $f_G(u) = F_{L(G)}(u)$.

Exact CBFGs are a more limited formalism than CBFGs themselves; without any limits on the interpretation of the features, we can define a class of formalisms that is equal to the class of Conjunctive Grammars (see Section 4). However, exactness is an important notion because it allows to associate intrinsic components of a language to strings. Contexts are easily observable from a sample and moreover it is only when the features correspond to the contexts that distributional learning algorithms can infer the structure of the language. A basic example of such a learning algorithm is given in (Clark et al., 2008).

3.2 A Parsing Example

To clarify the relationship with CFG parsing, we will give a simple worked example. Consider the CBFG $G = \langle \{(\lambda, \lambda), (aab, \lambda), (\lambda, b), (\lambda, abb), (a, \lambda)(aab, \lambda)\}, P, P_L, \{a, b\} \rangle$ with $P_L = \{\{(\lambda, b), (\lambda, abb)\} \to a, \{(a, \lambda), (aab, \lambda)\} \to b\}$ and $P = \{\{(\lambda, \lambda)\} \to \{(\lambda, b)\}\{(aab, \lambda)\}, \{(\lambda, \lambda)\} \to \{(\lambda, abb)\}\{(a, \lambda)\}, \{(\lambda, b)\} \to \{(\lambda, abb)\}\{(\lambda, \lambda)\}, \{(a, \lambda)\} \to \{(\lambda, \lambda)\}\{(aab, \lambda)\}\}$.

If we want to parse the string $w = aabb$ the usual way is to have a bottom-up approach. This means that we recursively compute the f_G map on the substrings of w in order to check whether (λ, λ) belongs to $f_G(w)$.

The Figure 1 graphically gives the main steps of the computation of $f_G(aabb)$. Basically there are two ways to split $aabb$ that allow the derivation of the empty context: $aab|b$ and $a|abb$. The first one correspond to the top part of the figure while the second one is drawn at the bottom. We can see for instance that the empty context belongs to $f_G(ab)$ thanks to the rule $\{(\lambda, \lambda)\} \to \{(\lambda, abb)\}\{(a, \lambda)\}$: $\{(\lambda, abb)\} \subseteq f_G(a)$ and $\{(a, \lambda)\} \subseteq f_G(b)$. But for symmetrical reasons the result can also be obtained using the rule $\{(\lambda, \lambda)\} \rightarrow \{(\lambda, b)\}\{(aab, \lambda)\}$.

As we trivially have $f_G(aa) = f_G(bb) = \emptyset$, since no right-hand side contains the concatenation of the same two features, an induction proof can be written to show that $(\lambda, \lambda) \in f_G(w) \Leftrightarrow w \in \{a^n b^n : n > 0\}$.

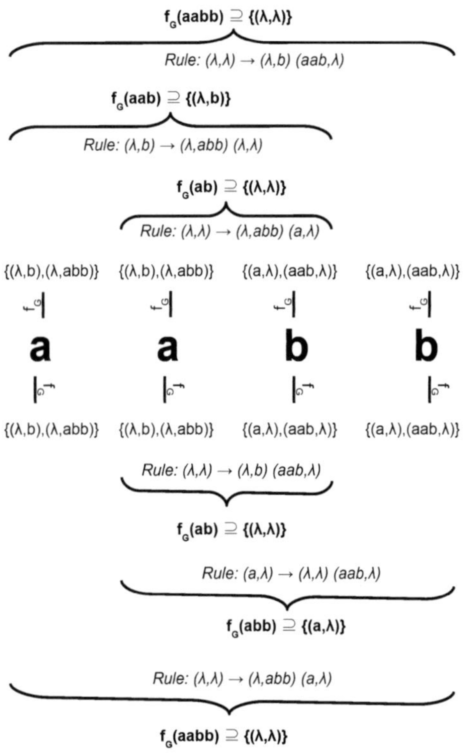

Figure 1: The two derivations to obtain (λ, λ) in $f_G(aabb)$ in the grammar G.

This is a simple example that illustrates the parsing of a string given a CBFG. This example does not characterize the power of CBFG since no right handside part is composed of more than one context. A more interesting, example with a context-sensitive language, will be presented in Section 7.

4 Non exact CBFGs

The aim here is to study the expressive power of CBFG compare to other formalism recently introduced. Though the inference can be done only for exact CBFG, where features are directly linked with observable contexts, it is still worth having a look at the more general characteristics of CBFG. For instance, it is interesting to note that several formalisms introduced with the aim of representing natural languages share strong links with CBFG.

Range Concatenation Grammars

Range Concatenation Grammars are a very powerful formalism (Boullier, 2000), that is a current area of research in NLP.

Lemma 3. *For every CBFG G, there is a non-erasing positive range concatenation grammar of arity one, in 2-var form that defines the same language.*

Proof. Suppose $G = \langle F, P, P_L, \Sigma \rangle$. Define a RCG with a set of predicates equal to F and the following clauses, and the two variables U, V. For each production $x \rightarrow yz$ in P, for each $f \in x$, where $y = \{g_1, \ldots g_i\}$, $z = \{h_1, \ldots h_j\}$ add clauses
$f(UV) \rightarrow g_1(U), \ldots g_i(U), h_1(V), \ldots h_j(V)$. For each lexical production $\{f_1 \ldots f_k\} \rightarrow a$ add clauses $f_i(a) \rightarrow \epsilon$. It is straightforward to verify that $f(w) \vdash \epsilon$ iff $f \in f_G(w)$. □

Conjunctive Grammar

A more exact correspondence is to the class of Conjunctive Grammars (Okhotin, 2001), invented independently of RCGs. For every every language L generated by a conjunctive grammar there is a CBFG representing $L\#$ (where the special character $\#$ is not included in the original alphabet).

Suppose we have a conjunctive grammar $G = \langle \Sigma, N, P, S \rangle$ in binary normal form (as defined in (Okhotin, 2003)). We construct the equivalent CBFG $G' = \langle F, P', P_L, \Sigma \rangle$ as followed:

- For every letter a we add a context (l_a, r_a) to F such that $l_a a r_a \in L$;
- For every rules $X \rightarrow a$ in P, we create a rule $\{(l_a, r_a)\} \rightarrow a$ in P_L.
- For every non terminal $X \in N$, for every rule $X \rightarrow P_1Q_1 \& \ldots \& P_nQ_n$ we add distinct contexts $\{(l_{P_iQ_i}, r_{P_iQ_i})\}$ to F, such that for all i it exists u_i, $l_{P_iQ_i} u_i r_{P_iQ_i} \in L$ and $P_iQ_i \stackrel{*}{\Rightarrow}_G u_i$;
- Let $F_{X,j} = \{(l_{P_iQ_i}, r_{P_iQ_i}) : \forall i\}$ the set of contexts corresponding to the jth rule applicable to X. For all

$(l_{P_iQ_i}, r_{P_iQ_i}) \in F_{X,j}$, we add to P' the rules $(l_{P_iQ_i}, r_{P_iQ_i}) \rightarrow F_{P_i,k}F_{Q_i,l}$ $(\forall k, l)$.

- We add a new context (w, λ) to F such that $S \stackrel{*}{\Rightarrow}_G w$ and $(w, \lambda) \rightarrow \#$ to P_L;
- For all j, we add to P' the rule $(\lambda, \lambda) \rightarrow F_{S,j}\{(w, \lambda)\}$.

It can be shown that this construction gives an equivalent CBFG.

5 Regular Languages

Any regular language can be defined by an exact CBFG. In order to show this we will propose an approach defining a canonical form for representing any regular language.

Suppose we have a regular language L, we consider the left and right residual languages:

$$u^{-1}L = \{w | uw \in L\} \tag{4}$$

$$Lu^{-1} = \{w | wu \in L\} \tag{5}$$

They define two congruencies: if $l, l' \in u^{-1}L$ (resp. $r, r' \in Lu^{-1}$) then for all $w \in \Sigma^*$, $lw \in L$ iff $l'w \in L$ (resp. $wr \in L$ iff $wr' \in L$).

For any $u \in \Sigma^*$, let $l_{min}(u)$ be the lexicographically shortest element such that $l_{min}^{-1}L = u^{-1}L$. The number of such l_{min} is finite by the Myhil-Nerode theorem, we denote by L_{min} this set, i.e. $\{l_{min}(u) | u \in \Sigma^*\}$. We define symmetrically R_{min} for the right residuals ($Lr_{min}^{-1} = Lu^{-1}$).

We define the set of contexts as:

$$F(L) = L_{min} \times R_{min}. \tag{6}$$

$F(L)$ is clearly finite by construction.

If we consider the regular language defined by the deterministic finite automata of Figure 2, we obtain $L_{min} = \{\lambda, a, b\}$ and $R_{min} = \{\lambda, b, ab\}$ and thus $F(L) = \{(\lambda, \lambda), (a, \lambda), (b, \lambda), (\lambda, b), (a, b), (b, b), (\lambda, ab), (a, ab), (b, ab)\}$.

By considering this set of features, we can prove (using arguments about congruence classes) that for any strings u, v such that $F_L(u) \supset F_L(v)$, then $C_L(u) \supset C_L(v)$. This means the set of feature F is sufficient to represent context inclusion, we call this property the *fiduciality*.

Note that the number of congruence classes of a regular language is finite. Each congruence class is represented by a set of contexts

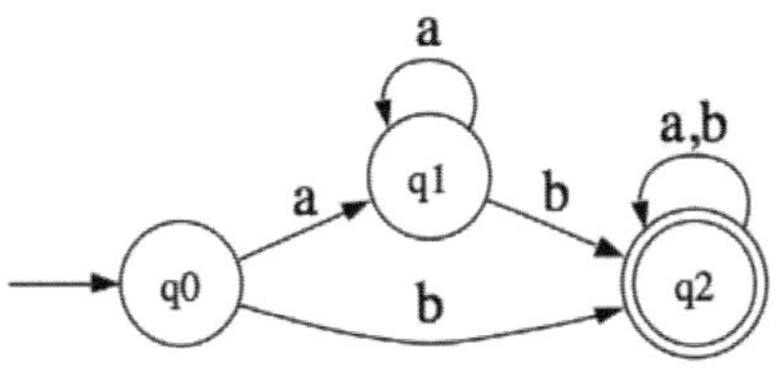

Figure 2: Example of a DFA. The left residuals are defined by $\lambda^{-1}L$, $a^{-1}L$, $b^{-1}L$ and the right ones by $L\lambda^{-1}$, Lb^{-1}, Lab^{-1} (note here that $La^{-1} = L\lambda^{-1}$).

$F_L(u)$. Let K_L be finite set of strings formed by taking the lexicographically shortest string from each congruence class. The final grammar can be obtained by combining elements of K_L. For every pair of strings $u, v \in K_L$, we define a rule

$$F_L(uv) \rightarrow F_L(u), F_L(v) \tag{7}$$

and we add lexical productions of the form $F_L(a) \rightarrow a$, $a \in \Sigma$.

Lemma 4. *For all $w \in \Sigma^*$, $f_G(w) = F_L(w)$.*

Proof. (Sketch) Proof in two steps: $\forall w \in \Sigma^*, F_L(w) \subseteq f_G(w)$ and $f_G(w) \subseteq F_L(w)$. Each step is made by induction on the length of w and uses the rules created to build the grammar, the derivation process of a CBFG and the fiduciality for the second step. The key point rely on the fact that when a string w is parsed by a CBFG G, there exists a cut of w in $uv = w$ ($u, v \in \Sigma^*$) and a rule $z \rightarrow xy$ in G such that $x \subseteq f_G(u)$ and $y \subseteq f_G(v)$. The rule $z \rightarrow xy$ is also obtained from a substring from the set used to build the grammar using the F_L map. By inductive hypothesis you obtain inclusion between f_G and F_L on u and v. □

For the language of Figure 2, the following set is sufficient to build an exact CBGF: $\{a, b, aa, ab, ba, aab, bb, bba\}$ (this corresponds to all the substrings of aab and bba). We have:

$F_L(a) = F(L) \backslash \{(\lambda, \lambda), (a, \lambda)\} \rightarrow a$

$F_L(b) = F(L) \rightarrow b$

$F_L(aa) = F_L(a) \rightarrow F_L(a), F_L(a)$

$F_L(ab) = F(L) \rightarrow F_L(a), F_L(b) = F_L(a), F(L)$

$F_L(ba) = F(L) \rightarrow F_L(b), F_L(a) = F(L), F_L(a)$

$F_L(bb) = F(L) \rightarrow F_L(b), F_L(b) = F(L), F(L)$

$F_L(aab) = F_L(bba) = F_L(ab) = F_L(ba)$

The approach presented here gives a canonical form for representing a regular language by an exact CBFG. Moreover, this is is *complete* in the sense that every context of every substring will be represented by some element of $F(L)$: this CBFG will completely model the relation between contexts and substrings.

6 Context-Free Languages

We now consider the relationship between CFGs and CBFGs.

Definition 5. *A context-free grammar (CFG) is a quadruple* $G = (\Sigma, V, P, S)$. Σ *is a finite alphabet,* V *is a set of non terminals* $(\Sigma \cap V = \emptyset)$, $P \subseteq V \times (V \cup \Sigma)^+$ *is a finite set of productions,* $S \in V$ *is the start symbol.*

In the following, we will suppose that a CFG is represented in Chomsky Normal Form, *i.e.* every production is in the form $N \rightarrow UW$ with $N, U, W \in V$ or $N \rightarrow a$ with $a \in \Sigma$.
We will write $uNv \Rightarrow_G u\alpha v$ if there is a production $N \rightarrow \alpha \in P$. $\stackrel{*}{\Rightarrow}_G$ is the reflexive transitive closure of $\Rightarrow_G$. The language defined by a CFG G is $L(G) = \{w \in \Sigma^* | S \stackrel{*}{\Rightarrow}_G w\}$.

6.1 A Simple Characterization

A simple approach to try to represent a CFG by a CBFG is to define a bijection between the set of non terminals and the set of context features. Informally we define each non terminal by a single context and rewrite the productions of the grammar in the CBFG form.

To build the set of contexts F, it is sufficient to choose $|V|$ contexts such that a bijection b_C can be defined between V and F with $b_C(N) = (l, r)$ implies that $S \stackrel{*}{\Rightarrow} lNr$. Note that we fix $b_T(S) = (\lambda, \lambda)$.

Then, we can define a CBFG $\langle F, P', P'_L, \Sigma\rangle$, where $P' = \{b_T(N) \rightarrow b_T(U)b_T(W) | N \rightarrow UW \in P\}$ and $P'_L = \{b_T(N) \rightarrow a | N \rightarrow a \in P, a \in \Sigma\}$. A similar proof showing that this construction produces an equivalent CBFG can be found in (Clark et al., 2008).

If this approach allows a simple syntactical convertion of a CFG into a CBFG, it is not relevant from an NLP point of view. Though we associate a non-terminal to a context, this may not correspond to the intrinsic property of the underlying language. A context could be associated with many non-terminals and we choose only one. For example, the context $(He\ is, \lambda)$ allows both noun phrases and adjective phrases. In formal terms, the resulting CBFG is not exact. Then, with the bijection we introduced before, we are not able to characterize the non-terminals by the contexts in which they could appear. This is clearly what we don't want here and we are more interested in the relationship with exact CBFG.

6.2 Not all CFLs have an exact CBFG

We will show here that the class of context-free grammars is not strictly included in the class of exact CBFGs. First, the grammar defined in Section 3.2 is an exact CBFG for the context-free and non regular language $\{a^n b^n | n > 0\}$, showing the class of exact CBFG has some elements in the class of CFGs.

We give now a context-free language L that can not be defined by an exact CBFG:

$$L = \{a^n b | n > 0\} \cup \{a^m c^n | n > m > 0\}.$$

Suppose that there exists an exact CBFG that recognizes it and let N be the length of the biggest feature (*i.e.* the longest left part of the feature). For any sufficiently large $k > N$, the sequences c^k and c^{k+1} share the same features: $F_L(c^k) = F_L(c^{k+1})$. Since the CBFG is exact we have $F_L(b) \subseteq F_L(c_k)$. Thus any derivation of $a^{k+1}b$ could be a derivation of $a^{k+1}c^k$ which does not belong to the language.

However, this restriction does not mean that the class of exact CBFG is too restrictive for modelling natural languages. Indeed, the example we have given is highly unnatural and such phenomena appear not to occur in attested natural languages.

7 Context-Sensitive Languages

We now show that there are some exact CBFGs that are not context-free. In particular, we define a language closely related to the *MIX language* (consisting of strings with an equal number of a's, b's and c's in any order) which is known to be non context-free, and indeed is conjectured to be outside the class of indexed grammars (Boullier, 2003).

Let $M = \{(a,b,c)^*\}$, we consider the language $L = L_{abc} \cup L_{ab} \cup L_{ac} \cup \{a'a, b'b, c'c, dd', ee', ff'\}$:
$L_{ab} = \{wd | w \in M, |w|_a = |w|_b\}$,
$L_{ac} = \{we | w \in M, |w|_a = |w|_c\}$,
$L_{abc} = \{wf | w \in M, |w|_a = |w|_b = |w|_c\}$.
In order to define a CBFG recognizing L, we have to select features (contexts) that can represent exactly the intrinsic components of the languages composing L. We propose to use the following set of features for each sublanguages:

- For L_{ab}: (λ, d) and $(\lambda, ad), (\lambda, bd)$.
- For L_{ac}: (λ, e) and $(\lambda, ae), (\lambda, ce)$.
- For L_{abc}: (λ, f).
- For the letters a', b', c', a, b, c we add: $(\lambda, a), (\lambda, b), (\lambda, c), (a', \lambda), (b', \lambda), (c', \lambda)$.
- For the letters d, e, f, d', e', f' we add; $(\lambda, d'), (\lambda, e'), (\lambda, f'), (d, \lambda), (e, \lambda), (f, \lambda)$.

Here, L_{ab} will be represented by (λ, d), but we will use $(\lambda, ad), (\lambda, bd)$ to define the internal derivations of elements of L_{ab}. The same idea holds for L_{ac} with (λ, e) and $(\lambda, ae), (\lambda, ce)$.

For the lexical rules and in order to have an exact CBFG, note the special case for a, b, c:
$\{(\lambda, bd), (\lambda, ce), (a', \lambda)\} \rightarrow a$
$\{(\lambda, ad), (b', \lambda)\} \rightarrow b$
$\{(\lambda, ad), (\lambda, ae), (c', \lambda)\} \rightarrow c$
For the nine other letters, each one is defined with only one context like $\{(\lambda, d')\} \rightarrow d$.

For the production rules, the most important one is: $(\lambda, \lambda) \rightarrow \{(\lambda, d), (\lambda, e)\}, \{(\lambda, f')\}$.

Indeed, this rule, with the presence of two contexts in one of categories, means that an element of the language has to be derived so that it has a prefix u such that $f_G(u) \supseteq \{(\lambda, d), (\lambda, e)\}$. This means u is both an element of L_{ab} and L_{ac}. This rule represents the language L_{abc} since $\{(\lambda, f')\}$ can only represent the letter f.

The other parts of the language will be defined by the following rules:
$(\lambda, \lambda) \rightarrow \{(\lambda, d)\}, \{(\lambda, d')\}$,
$(\lambda, \lambda) \rightarrow \{(\lambda, e)\}, \{(\lambda, e')\}$,
$(\lambda, \lambda) \rightarrow \{(\lambda, a)\}, \{(\lambda, bd), (\lambda, ce), (a', \lambda)\}$,
$(\lambda, \lambda) \rightarrow \{(\lambda, b)\}, \{(\lambda, ad), (b', \lambda)\}$,
$(\lambda, \lambda) \rightarrow \{(\lambda, c)\}, \{(\lambda, ad), (\lambda, ae), (c', \lambda)\}$,
$(\lambda, \lambda) \rightarrow \{(\lambda, d')\}, \{(d, \lambda)\}$,
$(\lambda, \lambda) \rightarrow \{(\lambda, e')\}, \{(e, \lambda)\}$,
$(\lambda, \lambda) \rightarrow \{(\lambda, f')\}, \{(f, \lambda)\}$.

This set of rules is incomplete, since for representing L_{ab}, the grammar must contain the rules ensuring to have the same number of a's and b's, and similarly for L_{ac}. To lighten the presentation here, the complete grammar is presented in Annex.

We claim this is an exact CBFG for a context-sensitive language. L is not context-free since if we intersect L with the regular language $\{\Sigma^* d\}$, we get an instance of the non context-free MIX language (with d appended). The exactness comes from the fact that we chose the contexts in order to ensure that strings belonging to a sublanguage can not belong to another one and that the derivation of a substring will provide all the possible correct features with the help of the union of all the possible derivations.

Note that the Mix language on its own is probably not definable by an exact CBFG: it is only when other parts of the language can distributionally define the appropriate partial structures that we can get context sensitive languages. Far from being a limitation of this formalism (a bug), we argue this is a feature: it is only in rather exceptional circumstances that we will get properly context sensitive languages. This formalism thus potentially accounts not just for the existence of non context free natural language but also for their rarity.

8 Conclusion

The chart in Figure 3 summarises the different relationship shown in this paper. The substitutable languages (Clark and Eyraud, 2007) and the very simple ones (Yokomori, 2003) form two different learnable class of languages. There is an interesting relationship with Marcus External Contextual Grammars (Mitrana, 2005): if we defined the language of a CBFG to be the set $\{f_G(u) \odot u : u \in \Sigma^*\}$ we would be taking some steps towards contextual grammars.

In this paper we have discussed the weak generative power of Exact Contextual Binary Feature Grammars; we conjecture that the class of natural language stringsets lie in this class. ECBFGs are efficiently learnable (see (Clark et al., 2008) for details) which is a com-

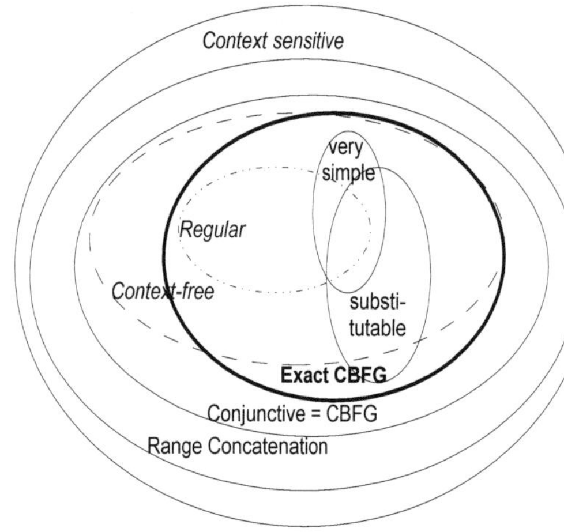

Figure 3: The relationship between CBFG and other classes of languages.

pelling technical advantage of this formalism over other more traditional formalisms such as CFGs or TAGs.

References

Pierre Boullier. 2000. A Cubic Time Extension of Context-Free Grammars. *Grammars*, 3:111–131.

Pierre Boullier. 2003. Counting with range concatenation grammars. *Theoretical Computer Science*, 293(2):391–416.

Alexander Clark and Rémi Eyraud. 2007. Polynomial identification in the limit of substitutable context-free languages. *Journal of Machine Learning Research*, 8:1725–1745, Aug.

Alexander Clark, Rémi Eyraud, and Amaury Habrard. 2008. A polynomial algorithm for the inference of context free languages. In *Proceedings of International Colloquium on Grammatical Inference*, pages 29–42. Springer, September.

V. Mitrana. 2005. Marcus external contextual grammars: From one to many dimensions. *Fundamenta Informaticae*, 54:307–316.

Alexander Okhotin. 2001. Conjunctive grammars. *J. Autom. Lang. Comb.*, 6(4):519–535.

Alexander Okhotin. 2003. An overview of conjunctive grammars. *Formal Language Theory Column, bulletin of the EATCS*, 79:145–163.

Takashi Yokomori. 2003. Polynomial-time identification of very simple grammars from positive data. *Theoretical Computer Science*, 298(1):179–206.

Annex

$$
\begin{array}{l}
(\lambda,\lambda) \rightarrow \{(\lambda,d),(\lambda,e)\},\{(\lambda,f')\} \\
(\lambda,\lambda) \rightarrow \{(\lambda,d)\},\{(\lambda,d')\} \\
(\lambda,\lambda) \rightarrow \{(\lambda,e)\},\{(\lambda,e')\} \\
(\lambda,\lambda) \rightarrow \{(\lambda,a)\},\{(\lambda,bd),(\lambda,ce),(a',\lambda)\} \\
(\lambda,\lambda) \rightarrow \{(\lambda,b)\},\{(\lambda,ad),(b',\lambda)\} \\
(\lambda,\lambda) \rightarrow \{(\lambda,c)\},\{(\lambda,ad),(\lambda,ae),(c',\lambda)\} \\
(\lambda,\lambda) \rightarrow \{(\lambda,d')\},\{(d,\lambda)\} \\
(\lambda,\lambda) \rightarrow \{(\lambda,e')\},\{(e,\lambda)\} \\
(\lambda,\lambda) \rightarrow \{(\lambda,f')\},\{(f,\lambda)\}
\end{array}
$$

$$
\begin{array}{l}
(\lambda,d) \rightarrow \{(\lambda,d)\},\{(\lambda,d)\} \\
(\lambda,d) \rightarrow \{(\lambda,ad)\},\{(\lambda,bd)\} \\
(\lambda,d) \rightarrow \{(\lambda,bd)\},\{(\lambda,ad)\} \\
(\lambda,d) \rightarrow \{(\lambda,d)\},\{(\lambda,ad),(\lambda,ae),(c',\lambda)\} \\
(\lambda,d) \rightarrow \{(\lambda,ad),(\lambda,ae),(c',\lambda)\},\{(\lambda,d)\}
\end{array}
$$

$$
\begin{array}{l}
(\lambda,ad) \rightarrow \{(\lambda,ad),(\lambda,ae),(c',\lambda)\},\{(\lambda,ad)\} \\
(\lambda,ad) \rightarrow \{(\lambda,ad)\},\{(\lambda,ad),(\lambda,ae),(c',\lambda)\} \\
(\lambda,ad) \rightarrow \{(\lambda,ad),(b',\lambda)\},\{(\lambda,d)\} \\
(\lambda,ad) \rightarrow \{(\lambda,d)\},\{(\lambda,ad),(b',\lambda)\}
\end{array}
$$

$$
\begin{array}{l}
(\lambda,bd) \rightarrow \{(\lambda,ad),(\lambda,ae),(c',\lambda)\},\{(\lambda,bd)\} \\
(\lambda,bd) \rightarrow \{(\lambda,bd)\},\{(\lambda,ad),(\lambda,ae),(c',\lambda)\} \\
(\lambda,bd) \rightarrow \{(\lambda,bd),(\lambda,ce),(a',\lambda)\},\{(\lambda,d)\} \\
(\lambda,bd) \rightarrow \{(\lambda,d)\},\{(\lambda,bd),(\lambda,ce),(a',\lambda)\} \\
(\lambda,e) \rightarrow \{(\lambda,e)\},\{(\lambda,e)\} \\
(\lambda,e) \rightarrow \{(\lambda,ae)\},\{(\lambda,ce)\} \\
(\lambda,e) \rightarrow \{(\lambda,ce)\},\{(\lambda,ae)\} \\
(\lambda,e) \rightarrow \{(\lambda,e)\},\{(\lambda,ad),(b',\lambda)\} \\
(\lambda,e) \rightarrow \{(\lambda,ad),(b',\lambda)\},\{(\lambda,e)\} \\
(\lambda,ae) \rightarrow \{(\lambda,ad),(b',\lambda)\},\{(\lambda,ae)\} \\
(\lambda,ae) \rightarrow \{(\lambda,ae)\},\{(\lambda,ad),(b',\lambda)\} \\
(\lambda,ae) \rightarrow \{(\lambda,ad),(\lambda,ae),(c',\lambda)\},\{(\lambda,e)\} \\
(\lambda,ae) \rightarrow \{(\lambda,e)\},\{(\lambda,ad),(\lambda,ae),(c',\lambda)\} \\
(\lambda,ce) \rightarrow \{(\lambda,ad),(b',\lambda)\},\{(\lambda,ce)\} \\
(\lambda,ce) \rightarrow \{(\lambda,ce)\},\{(\lambda,ad),(b',\lambda)\} \\
(\lambda,ce) \rightarrow \{(\lambda,bd),(\lambda,ce),(a',\lambda)\},\{(\lambda,e)\} \\
(\lambda,ce) \rightarrow \{(\lambda,e)\},\{(\lambda,bd),(\lambda,ce),(a',\lambda)\} \\
\{(\lambda,bd),(\lambda,ce),(a',\lambda)\} \rightarrow a \\
\{(\lambda,ad),(b',\lambda)\} \rightarrow b \\
\{(\lambda,ad),(\lambda,ae),(c',\lambda)\} \rightarrow c \\
\{(\lambda,d')\} \rightarrow d \\
\{(\lambda,e')\} \rightarrow e \\
\{(\lambda,f')\} \rightarrow f \\
\{(\lambda,a)\} \rightarrow a' \\
\{(\lambda,b)\} \rightarrow b' \\
\{(\lambda,c)\} \rightarrow c' \\
\{(d,\lambda)\} \rightarrow d' \\
\{(e,\lambda)\} \rightarrow e' \\
\{(f,\lambda)\} \rightarrow f'
\end{array}
$$

Language models for contextual error detection and correction

Herman Stehouwer
Tilburg Centre for Creative Computing
Tilburg University
Tilburg, The Netherlands
j.h.stehouwer@uvt.nl

Menno van Zaanen
Tilburg Centre for Creative Computing
Tilburg University
Tilburg, The Netherlands
mvzaanen@uvt.nl

Abstract

The problem of identifying and correcting confusibles, i.e. context-sensitive spelling errors, in text is typically tackled using specifically trained machine learning classifiers. For each different set of confusibles, a specific classifier is trained and tuned.

In this research, we investigate a more generic approach to context-sensitive confusible correction. Instead of using specific classifiers, we use one generic classifier based on a language model. This measures the likelihood of sentences with different possible solutions of a confusible in place. The advantage of this approach is that all confusible sets are handled by a single model. Preliminary results show that the performance of the generic classifier approach is only slightly worse that that of the specific classifier approach.

1 Introduction

When writing texts, people often use spelling checkers to reduce the number of spelling mistakes in their texts. Many spelling checkers concentrate on non-word errors. These errors can be easily identified in texts because they consist of character sequences that are not part of the language. For example, in English *woord* is is not part of the language, hence a non-word error. A possible correction would be *word*.

Even when a text does not contain any non-word errors, there is no guarantee that the text is error-free. There are several types of spelling errors where the words themselves are part of the language, but are used incorrectly in their context. Note that these kinds of errors are much harder to recognize, as information from the context in which they occur is required to recognize and correct these errors. In contrast, non-word errors can be recognized without context.

One class of such errors, called *confusibles*, consists of words that belong to the language, but are used incorrectly with respect to their local, sentential context. For example, *She owns to cars* contains the confusible *to*. Note that this word is a valid token and part of the language, but used incorrectly in the context. Considering the context, a correct and very likely alternative would be the word *two*. Confusibles are grouped together in confusible sets. Confusible sets are sets of words that are similar and often used incorrectly in context. *Too* is the third alternative in this particular confusible set.

The research presented here is part of a larger project, which focusses on context-sensitive spelling mistakes in general. Within this project all classes of context-sensitive spelling errors are tackled. For example, in addition to confusibles, a class of pragmatically incorrect words (where words are incorrectly used within the document-wide context) is considered as well. In this article we concentrate on the problem of confusibles, where the context is only as large as a sentence.

2 Approach

A typical approach to the problem of confusibles is to train a machine learning classifier to a specific confusible set. Most of the work in this area has concentrated on confusibles due to homophony (*to*, *too*, *two*) or similar spelling (*desert*, *dessert*). However, some research has also touched upon inflectional or derivational confusibles such as *I* versus *me* (Golding and Roth, 1999). For instance, when word forms are homophonic, they tend to get confused often in writing (cf. the situation with *to*, *too*, and *two*, *affect* and *effect*, or *there*, *their*, and *they're* in English) (Sandra et al., 2001; Van den Bosch and Daelemans, 2007).

Proceedings of the EACL 2009 Workshop on Computational Linguistic Aspects of Grammatical Inference, pages 41–48,
Athens, Greece, 30 March 2009. ©2009 Association for Computational Linguistics

Most work on confusible disambiguation using machine learning concentrates on hand-selected sets of notorious confusibles. The confusible sets are typically very small (two or three elements) and the machine learner will only see training examples of the members of the confusible set. This approach is similar to approaches used in accent restoration (Yarowsky, 1994; Golding, 1995; Mangu and Brill, 1997; Wu et al., 1999; Even-Zohar and Roth, 2000; Banko and Brill, 2001; Huang and Powers, 2001; Van den Bosch, 2006).

The task of the machine learner is to decide, using features describing information from the context, which word taken from the confusible set really belongs in the position of the confusible. Using the example above, the classifier has to decide which word belongs on the position of the **X** in *She owns* **X** *cars*, where the possible answers for **X** are *to*, *too*, or *two*. We call **X**, the confusible that is under consideration, the *focus word*.

Another way of looking at the problem of confusible disambiguation is to see it as a very specialized case of word prediction. The problem is then to predict which word belongs at a specific position. Using similarities between these cases, we can use techniques from the field of language modeling to solve the problem of selecting the best alternative from confusible sets. We will investigate this approach in this article.

Language models assign probabilities to sequences of words. Using this information, it is possible to predict the most likely word in a certain context. If a language model gives us the probability for a sequence of n words $P_{LM}(w_1, \ldots, w_n)$, we can use this to predict the most likely word w following a sequence of $n-1$ words $\arg\max_w P_{LM}(w_1, \ldots, w_{n-1}, w)$. Obviously, a similar approach can be taken with w in the middle of the sequence.

Here, we will use a language model as a classifier to predict the correct word in a context. Since a language model models the entire language, it is different from a regular machine learning classifier trained on a specific set of confusibles. The advantage of this approach to confusible disambiguation is that the language model can handle all potential confusibles without any further training and tuning. With the language model it is possible to take the words from any confusible set and compute the probabilities of those words in the context. The element from the confusible set that has the highest probability according to the language model is then selected. Since the language model assigns probabilities to all sequences of words, it is possible to define new confusible sets on the fly and let the language model disambiguate them without any further training. Obviously, this is not possible for a specialized machine learning classifier approach, where a classifier is fine-tuned to the features and classes of a specific confusible set.

The expected disadvantage of the generic (language model) classifier approach is that the accuracy is expected to be less than that of the specific (specialized machine learning classifier) approach. Since the specific classifiers are tuned to each specific confusible set, the weights for each of the features may be different for each set. For instance, there may be confusibles for which the correct word is easily identified by words in a specific position. If a determiner, like *the*, occurs in the position directly before the confusible, *to* or *too* are very probably not the correct answers. The specific approach can take this into account by assigning specific weights to part-of-speech and position combinations, whereas the generic approach cannot do this explicitly for specific cases; the weights follow automatically from the training corpus.

In this article, we will investigate whether it is possible to build a confusible disambiguation system that is generic for all sets of confusibles using language models as generic classifiers and investigate in how far this approach is useful for solving the confusible problem. We will compare these generic classifiers against specific classifiers that are trained for each confusible set independently.

3 Results

To measure the effectiveness of the generic classifier approach to confusible disambiguation, and to compare it against a specific classifier approach we have implemented several classification systems. First of these is a majority class baseline system, which selects the word from the confusible set that occurs most often in the training data.[1] We have also implemented several generic classifiers based on different language models. We compare these against two machine learning classifiers. The machine learning classifiers are trained separately for each different experiment, whereas

[1]This baseline system corresponds to the simplest language model classifier. In this case, it only uses n-grams with $n = 1$.

the parameters and the training material of the language model are kept fixed throughout all the experiments.

3.1 System description

There are many different approaches that can be taken to develop language models. A well-known approach is to use n-grams, or Markov models. These models take into account the probability that a word occurs in the context of the previous $n-1$ words. The probabilities can be extracted from the occurrences of words in a corpus. Probabilities are computed by taking the relative occurrence count of the n words in sequence.

In the experiments described below, we will use a tri-gram-based language model and where required this model will be extended with bi-gram and uni-gram language models. The probability of a sequence is computed as the combination of the probabilities of the tri-grams that are found in the sequence.

Especially when n-grams with large n are used, data sparseness becomes an issue. The training data may not contain any occurrences of the particular sequence of n symbols, even though the sequence is correct. In that case, the probability extracted from the training data will be zero, even though the correct probability should be non-zero (albeit small). To reduce this problem we can either use back-off or smoothing when the probability of an n-gram is zero. In the case of back-off, the probabilities of lower order n-grams are taken into account when needed. Alternatively, smoothing techniques (Chen and Goodman, 1996) redistribute the probabilities, taking into account previously unseen word sequences.

Even though the language models provide us with probabilities of entire sequences, we are only interested in the n-grams directly around the confusible when using the language models in the context of confusible disambiguation. The probabilities of the rest of the sequence will remain the same whichever alternative confusible is inserted in the focus word position. Figure 1 illustrates that the probability of for example P(*analysts had expected*) is irrelevant for the decision between *then* and *than* because it occurs in both sequences.

The different language models we will consider here are essentially the same. The differences lie in how they handle sequences that have zero probability. Since the probabilities of the n-grams are multiplied, having a n-gram probability of zero results in a zero probability for the entire sequence. There may be two reasons for an n-gram to have probability zero: there is not enough training data, so this sequence has not been seen yet, or this sequence is not valid in the language.

When it is known that a sequence is not valid in the language, this information can be used to decide which word from the confusible set should be selected. However, when the sequence simply has not been seen in the training data yet, we cannot rely on this information. To resolve the sequences with zero probability, we can use smoothing. However, this assumes that the sequence is valid, but has not been seen during training. The other solution, back-off, tries not to make this assumption. It checks whether subsequences of the sequence are valid, i.e. have non-zero probabilities. Because of this, we will not use smoothing to reach non-zero probabilities in the current experiments, although this may be investigated further in the future.

The first language model that we will investigate here is a linear combination of the different n-grams. The probability of a sequence is computed by a linear combination of weighted n-gram probabilities. We will report on two different weight settings, one system using uniform weighting, called *uniform linear*, and one where uni-grams receive weight 1, bi-grams weight 138, and tri-grams weight 437.[2] These weights are normalized to yield a final probability for the sequence, resulting in the second system called *weighted linear*.

The third system uses the probabilities of the different n-grams separately, instead of using the probabilities of all n-grams at the same time as is done in the linear systems. The *continuous back-off* method uses only one of the probabilities at each position, preferring the higher-level probabilities. This model provides a step-wise back-off. The probability of a sequence is that of the tri-grams contained in that sequence. However, if the probability of a trigram is zero, a back-off to the probabilities of the two bi-grams of the sequence is used. If that is still zero, the uni-gram probability at that position is used. Note that this uni-gram probability is exactly what the baseline system

[2]These weights are selected by computing the accuracy of all combinations of weights on a held out set.

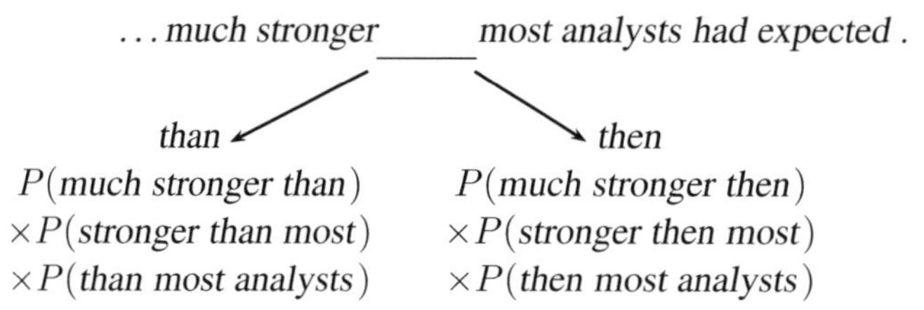

Figure 1: Computation of probabilities using the language model.

uses. With this approach it may be the case that the probability for one word in the confusible set is computed based on tri-grams, whereas the probability of another word in the set of confusibles is based on bi-grams or even the uni-gram probability. Effectively, this means that different kinds of probabilities are compared. The same weights as in the weighted linear systems are used.

To resolve the problem of unbalanced probabilities, a fourth language model, called *synchronous back-off*, is proposed. Whereas in the case of the continuous back-off model, two words from the confusible set may be computed using probabilities of different level n-grams, the synchronous back-off model uses probabilities of the same level of n-grams for all words in the confusible set, with n being the highest value for which at least one of the words has a non-zero probability. For instance, when word a has a tri-gram probability of zero and word b has a non-zero tri-gram probability, b is selected. When both have a zero tri-gram probability, a back-off to bi-grams is performed for both words. This is in line with the idea that if a probability is zero, the training data is sufficient, hence the sequence is not in the language.

To implement the specific classifiers, we used the TiMBL implementation of a k-NN classifier (Daelemans et al., 2007). This implementation of the k-NN algorithm is called *IB1*. We have tuned the different parameter settings for the k-NN classifier using Paramsearch (Van den Bosch, 2004), which resulted in a k of 35.[3] To describe the instances, we try to model the data as similar as possible to the data used by the generic classifier approach. Since the language model approaches use n-grams with $n = 3$ as the largest n, the features for the specific classifier approach use words one and two positions left and right of the focus word. The focus word becomes the class that needs to be predicted. We show an example of both training and testing in figure 2. Note that the features for the machine learning classifiers could be expanded with, for instance, part-of-speech tags, but in the current experiments only the word forms are used as features.

In addition to the k-NN classifier, we also run the experiments using the IGTree classifier, which is denoted *IGTree* in the rest of the article, which is also contained in the TiMBL distribution. IGTree is a fast, trie based, approximation of k-nearest neighbor classification (Knuth, 1973; Daelemans et al., 1997). IGTree allows for fast training and testing even with millions of examples. IGTree compresses a set of labeled examples into a decision tree structure similar to the classic C4.5 algorithm (Quinlan, 1993), except that throughout one level in the IGTree decision tree, the same feature is tested. Classification in IGTree is a simple procedure in which the decision tree is traversed from the root node down, and one path is followed that matches the actual values of the new example to be classified. If a leaf is found, the outcome stored at the leaf of the IGTree is returned as the classification. If the last node is not a leaf node, but there are no outgoing arcs that match a feature-value combination of the instance, the most likely outcome stored at that node is produced as the resulting classification. This outcome is computed by collating the outcomes of all leaf nodes that can be reached from the node.

IGTree is typically able to compress a large example set into a lean decision tree with high compression factors. This is done in reasonably short time, comparable to other compression algorithms. More importantly, IGTree's classification time depends only on the number of features ($O(f)$). Indeed, in our experiments we observe high compression rates. One of the unique characteristics of IGTree compared to basic k-NN is its resemblance to smoothing of a basic language

[3]We note that k is handled slightly differently in TiMBL than usual, k denotes the number of closest distances considered. So if there are multiple instances that have the same (closest) distance they are all considered.

Training ... *much stronger* <u>*than*</u> *most analysts had expected .*

↓

$\langle$*much, stronger, most, analysts*$\rangle \Rightarrow$*than*

Testing ... *much stronger* ______ *most analysts had expected .*

↓

$\langle$*much, stronger, most, analysts*$\rangle \Rightarrow ?$

Figure 2: During training, a classified instance (in this case for the confusible pair {*then*, *than*}) are generated from a sentence. During testing, a similar instance is generated. The classifier decides what the corresponding class, and hence, which word should be the focus word.

model (Zavrel and Daelemans, 1997), while still being a generic classifier that supports any number and type of features. For these reasons, IGTree is also included in the experiments.

3.2 Experimental settings

The probabilities used in the language models of the generic classifiers are computed by looking at occurrences of n-grams. These occurrences are extracted from a corpus. The training instances used in the specific machine learning classifiers are also extracted from the same data set. For training purposes, we used the Reuters news corpus RCV1 (Lewis et al., 2004). The Reuters corpus contains about 810,000 categorized newswire stories as published by Reuters in 1996 and 1997. This corpus contains around 130 million tokens.

For testing purposes, we used the Wall Street Journal part of the Penn Treebank corpus (Marcus et al., 1993). This well-known corpus contains articles from the Wall Street Journal in 1987 to 1989. We extract our test-instances from this corpus in the same way as we extract our training data from the Reuters corpus. There are minor tokenization differences between the corpora. The data is corrected for these differences.

Both corpora are in the domain of English language news texts, so we expect them to have similar properties. However, they are different corpora and hence are slightly different. This means that there are also differences between the training and testing set. We have selected this division to create a more realistic setting. This should allow for a more to real-world use comparison than when both training and testing instances are extracted from the same corpus.

For the specific experiments, we selected a number of well-known confusible sets to test the different approaches. In particular, we look at {*then, than*}, {*its, it's*}, {*your, you're*}, {*their, there, they're*}. To compare the difficulty of these problems, we also selected two words at random and used them as a confusible set.

The random category consists of two words that where randomly selected from all words in the Reuters corpus that occurred more than a thousand times. The words that where chosen, and used for all experiments here are *refugees* and *effect*. They occur around 27 thousand times in the Reuters corpus.

3.3 Empirical results

Table 1 sums up the results we obtained with the different systems. The baseline scores are generally very high, which tells us that the distribution of classes in a single confusible set is severely skewed, up to a ten to one ratio. This also makes the task hard. There are many examples for one word in the set, but only very few training instances for the other(s). However, it is especially important to recognize the important aspects of the minority class.

The results clearly show that the specific classifier approaches outperform the other systems. For instance, on the first task ({*then, than*}) the classifier achieves an accuracy slightly over 98%, whereas the language model systems only yield around 96%. This is as expected. The classifier is trained on just one confusible task and is therefore able to specialize on that task.

Comparing the two specific classifiers, we see that the accuracy achieved by IB1 and IGTree is quite similar. In general, IGTree performs a bit worse than IB1 on all confusible sets, which is as expected. However, in general it is possible for IGTree to outperform IB1 on certain tasks. In our experience this mainly happens on tasks where the usage of IGTree, allowing for more compact internal representations, allows one to use much more training data. IGTree also leads to improved

	{*then, than*}	{*its, it's*}	{*your, you're*}	{*their, there, they're*}	random
Baseline	82.63	92.42	78.55	68.36	93.16
IB1	98.01	98.67	96.36	97.12	97.89
IGTree	97.07	96.75	96.00	93.02	95.79
Uniform linear	68.27	50.70	31.64	32.72	38.95
Weighted linear	94.43	92.88	93.09	93.25	88.42
Continuous back-off	81.49	83.22	74.18	86.01	63.68
Synchronous back-off	96.42	94.10	92.36	93.06	87.37
Number of cases	2,458	4,830	275	3,053	190

Table 1: This table shows the performance achieved by the different systems, shown in accuracy (%). The *Number of cases* denotes the number of instances in the testset.

performance in cases where the features have a strong, absolute ordering of importance with respect to the classification problem at hand.

The generic language model approaches perform reasonably well. However, there are clear differences between the approaches. For instance the weighted linear and synchronous back-off approaches work well, but uniform linear and continuous back-off perform much worse. Especially the synchronous back-off approach achieves decent results, regardless of the confusible problem.

It is not very surprising to see that the continuous back-off method performs worse than the synchronous back-off method. Remember that the continuous back-off method always uses lower level n-grams when zero probabilities are found. This is done independently of the probabilities of the other words in the confusible set. The continuous back-off method prefers n-grams with larger n, however it does not penalize backing off to an n-gram with smaller n. Combine this with the fact that n-gram probabilities with large n are comparatively lower than those for n-grams with smaller n and it becomes likely that a bi-gram contributes more to the erroneous option than the correct tri-gram does to the correct option. Tri-grams are more sparse than bi-grams, given the same data.

The weighted linear approach outperforms the uniform linear approach by a large margin on all confusible sets. It is likely that the contribution from the n-grams with large n overrules the probabilities of the n-grams with smaller n in the uniform linear method. This causes a bias towards the more frequent words, compounded by the fact that bi-grams, and uni-grams even more so, are less sparse and therefore contribute more to the total probability.

We see that the both generic and specific classifier approaches perform consistently across the different confusible sets. The synchronous back-off approach is the best performing generic classifier approach we tested. It consistently outperforms the baseline, and overall performs better than the weighted linear approach.

The experiments show that generic classifiers based on language model can be used in the context of confusible disambiguation. However, the n in the different n-grams is of major importance. Exactly which n grams should be used to compute the probability of a sequence requires more research. The experiments also show that approaches that concentrate on n-grams with larger n yield more encouraging results.

4 Conclusion and future work

Confusibles are spelling errors that can only be detected within their sentential context. This kind of errors requires a completely different approach compared to non-word errors (errors that can be identified out of context, i.e. sequences of characters that do not belong to the language). In practice, most confusible disambiguation systems are based on machine learning classification techniques, where for each type of confusible, a new classifier is trained and tuned.

In this article, we investigate the use of language models in the context of confusible disambiguation. This approach works by selecting the word in the set of confusibles that has the highest probability in the sentential context according to the language model. Any kind of language model can be used in this approach.

The main advantage of using language models as generic classifiers is that it is easy to add new sets of confusibles without retraining or adding additional classifiers. The entire language is modeled, which means that all the information on words in their context is inherently present.

The experiments show that using generic classifiers based on simple n-gram language models yield slightly worse results compared to the specific classifier approach, where each classifier is specifically trained on one confusible set. However, the advantage of the generic classifier approach is that only one system has to be trained, compared to different systems for each confusible in the specific classifier case. Also, the exact computation of the probabilities using the n-grams, in particular the means of backing-off, has a large impact on the results.

As future work, we would like to investigate the accuracy of more complex language models used as classifiers. The n-gram language models described here are relatively simple, but more complex language models could improve performance. In particular, instead of back-off, smoothing techniques could be investigated to reduce the impact of zero probability problems (Chen and Goodman, 1996). This assumes that the training data we are currently working with is not enough to properly describe the language.

Additionally, language models that concentrate on more structural descriptions of the language, for instance, using grammatical inference techniques (de la Higuera, 2005), or models that explicitly take long distance dependencies into account (Griffiths et al., 2005) can be investigated. This leads to much richer language models that could, for example, check whether there is already a verb in the sentence (which helps in cases such as {*its*, *it's*}).

A different route which we would also like to investigate is the usage of a specific classifier, such as TiMBL's IGTree, as a language model. If a classifier is trained to predict the next word in the sentence or to predict the word at a given position with both left and right context as features, it can be used to estimate the probability of the words in a confusible set, just like the language models we have looked at so far. Another type of classifier might estimate the perplexity at a position, or provide some other measure of "surprisedness". Effectively, these approaches all take a model of the entire language (as described in the training data) into account.

References

Banko, M. and Brill, E. (2001). Scaling to very very large corpora for natural language disambiguation. In *Proceedings of the 39th Annual Meeting of the Association for Computational Linguistics*, pages 26–33. Association for Computational Linguistics.

Chen, S. and Goodman, J. (1996). An empirical study of smoothing techniques for language modelling. In *Proceedings of the 34th Annual Meeting of the ACL*, pages 310–318. ACL.

Daelemans, W., Van den Bosch, A., and Weijters, A. (1997). IGTree: using trees for compression and classification in lazy learning algorithms. *Artificial Intelligence Review*, 11:407–423.

Daelemans, W., Zavrel, J., Van der Sloot, K., and Van den Bosch, A. (2007). TiMBL: Tilburg Memory Based Learner, version 6.1, reference guide. Technical Report ILK 07-07, ILK Research Group, Tilburg University.

de la Higuera, C. (2005). A bibliographical study of grammatical inference. *Pattern Recognition*, 38(9):1332 – 1348. Grammatical Inference.

Even-Zohar, Y. and Roth, D. (2000). A classification approach to word prediction. In *Proceedings of the First North-American Conference on Computational Linguistics*, pages 124–131, New Brunswick, NJ. ACL.

Golding, A. and Roth, D. (1999). A Winnow-Based Approach to Context-Sensitive Spelling Correction. *Machine Learning*, 34(1–3):107–130.

Golding, A. R. (1995). A Bayesian hybrid method for context-sensitive spelling correction. In *Proceedings of the 3rd workshop on very large corpora, ACL-95*.

Griffiths, T. L., Steyvers, M., Blei, D. M., and Tenenbaum, J. B. (2005). Integrating topics and syntax. In *In Advances in Neural Information Processing Systems 17*, pages 537–544. MIT Press.

Huang, J. H. and Powers, D. W. (2001). Large scale experiments on correction of confused words. In *Australasian Computer Science Conference Proceedings*, pages 77–82, Queensland AU. Bond University.

Knuth, D. E. (1973). *The art of computer programming*, volume 3: Sorting and searching. Addison-Wesley, Reading, MA.

Lewis, D. D., Yang, Y., Rose, T. G., Dietterich, G., Li, F., and Li, F. (2004). Rcv1: A new benchmark collection for text categorization research. *Journal of Machine Learning Research*, 5:361–397.

Mangu, L. and Brill, E. (1997). Automatic rule acquisition for spelling correction. In *Proceedings of the International Conference on Machine Learning*, pages 187–194.

Marcus, M., Santorini, S., and Marcinkiewicz, M. (1993). Building a Large Annotated Corpus of English: the Penn Treebank. *Computational Linguistics*, 19(2):313–330.

Quinlan, J. (1993). C4.5*: Programs for Machine Learning*. Morgan Kaufmann, San Mateo, CA.

Sandra, D., Daems, F., and Frisson, S. (2001). Zo helder en toch zoveel fouten! wat leren we uit psycholinguïstisch onderzoek naar werkwoordfouten bij ervaren spellers? *Tijdschrift van de Vereniging voor het Onderwijs in het Nederlands*, 30(3):3–20.

Van den Bosch, A. (2004). Wrapped progressive sampling search for optimizing learning algorithm parameters. In Verbrugge, R., Taatgen, N., and Schomaker, L., editors, *Proceedings of the Sixteenth Belgian-Dutch Conference on Artificial Intelligence*, pages 219–226, Groningen, The Netherlands.

Van den Bosch, A. (2006). Scalable classification-based word prediction and confusible correction. *Traitement Automatique des Langues*, 46(2):39–63.

Van den Bosch, A. and Daelemans, W. (2007). *Tussen Taal, Spelling en Onderwijs*, chapter Dat gebeurd mei niet: Computationele modellen voor verwarbare homofonen, pages 199–210. Academia Press.

Wu, D., Sui, Z., and Zhao, J. (1999). An information-based method for selecting feature types for word prediction. In *Proceedings of the Sixth European Conference on Speech Communication and Technology, EUROSPEECH'99*, Budapest.

Yarowsky, D. (1994). Decision lists for lexical ambiguity resolution: application to accent restoration in Spanish and French. In *Proceedings of the Annual Meeting of the ACL*, pages 88–95.

Zavrel, J. and Daelemans, W. (1997). Memory-based learning: Using similarity for smoothing. In *Proceedings of the 35th Annual Meeting of the Association for Computational Linguistics*, pages 436–443.

On statistical parsing of French with supervised and semi-supervised strategies

Marie Candito*, Benoît Crabbé* and Djamé Seddah◇

* Université Paris 7
UFRL et INRIA (Alpage)
30 rue du Château des Rentiers
F-75013 Paris — France

◇ Université Paris 4
LALIC et INRIA (Alpage)
28 rue Serpente
F-75006 Paris — France

Abstract

This paper reports results on grammatical induction for French. We investigate how to best train a parser on the French Treebank (Abeillé et al., 2003), viewing the task as a trade-off between generalizability and interpretability. We compare, for French, a supervised lexicalized parsing algorithm with a semi-supervised unlexicalized algorithm (Petrov et al., 2006) along the lines of (Crabbé and Candito, 2008). We report the best results known to us on French statistical parsing, that we obtained with the semi-supervised learning algorithm. The reported experiments can give insights for the task of grammatical learning for a morphologically-rich language, with a relatively limited amount of training data, annotated with a rather flat structure.

1 Natural language parsing

Despite the availability of annotated data, there have been relatively few works on French statistical parsing. Together with a treebank, the availability of several supervised or semi-supervised grammatical learning algorithms, primarily set up on English data, allows us to figure out how they behave on French.

Before that, it is important to describe the characteristics of the parsing task. In the case of statistical parsing, two different aspects of syntactic structures are to be considered : their capacity to capture regularities and their interpretability for further processing.

Generalizability Learning for statistical parsing requires structures that capture best the underlying regularities of the language, in order to apply these patterns to unseen data.

Since capturing underlying linguistic rules is also an objective for linguists, it makes sense to use supervised learning from linguistically-defined generalizations. One generalization is typically the use of phrases, and phrase-structure rules that govern the way words are grouped together. It has to be stressed that these syntactic rules exist at least in part independently of semantic interpretation.

Interpretability But the main reason to use supervised learning for parsing, is that we want structures that are as *interpretable* as possible, in order to extract some knowledge from the analysis (such as deriving a semantic analysis from a parse). Typically, we need a syntactic analysis to reflect how words *relate* to each other. This is our main motivation to use supervised learning : the learnt parser will output structures as defined by linguists-annotators, and thus interpretable within the linguistic theory underlying the annotation scheme of the treebank. It is important to stress that this is more than capturing syntactic regularities : it has to do with the *meaning* of the words.

It is not certain though that both requirements (generalizability / interpretability) are best met in the same structures. In the case of supervised learning, this leads to investigate different instantiations of the training trees, to help the learning, while keeping the maximum interpretability of the trees. As we will see with some of our experiments, it may be necessary to find a trade-off between generalizability and interpretability.

Further, it is not guaranteed that syntactic rules infered from a manually annotated treebank produce the best language model. This leads to

Proceedings of the EACL 2009 Workshop on Computational Linguistic Aspects of Grammatical Inference, pages 49–57,
Athens, Greece, 30 March 2009. ©2009 Association for Computational Linguistics

methods that use semi-supervised techniques on a treebank-infered grammar backbone, such as (Matsuzaki et al., 2005; Petrov et al., 2006).

The plan of the paper is as follows : in the next section, we describe the available treebank for French, and how its structures can be interpreted. In section 3, we describe the typical problems encountered when parsing using a plain probabilistic context-free grammar, and existing algorithmic solutions that try to circumvent these problems. Next we describe experiments and results when training parsers on the French data. Finally, we discuss related work and conclude.

2 Interpreting the French trees

The French Treebank (Abeillé et al., 2003) is a publicly available sample from the newspaper *Le Monde*, syntactically annotated and manually corrected for French.

```
<SENT>
  <NP fct="SUJ">
    <w cat="D" lemma="le" mph="ms" subcat="def">le</w>
    <w cat="N" lemma="bilan" mph="ms" subcat="C">bilan</w>
  </NP>
  <VN>
    <w cat="ADV" lemma="ne" subcat="neg">n'</w>
    <w cat="V" lemma="être" mph="P3s" subcat="">est</w>
  </VN>
  <AdP fct="MOD">
    <w compound="yes" cat="ADV" lemma="peut-être">
       <w catint="V">peut</w>
       <w catint="PONCT">-</w>
       <w catint="V">être</w>
    </w>
    <w cat="ADV" lemma="pas" subcat="neg">pas</w>
  </AdP>
  <AP fct="ATS">
    <w cat="ADV" lemma="aussi">aussi</w>
    <w cat="A" lemma="sombre" mph="ms" subcat="qual">sombre</w>
  </AP>
  <w cat="PONCT" lemma="." subcat="S">.</w>
</SENT>
```

Figure 1: Simplified example of the FTB

To encode syntactic information, it uses a combination of labeled constituents, morphological annotations and functional annotation for verbal dependents as illustrated in Figure 1. This constituent and functional annotation was performed in two successive steps : though the original release (Abeillé et al., 2000) consists of 20,648 sentences (hereafter FTB-V0), the functional annotation was performed later on a subset of 12351 sentences (hereafter FTB). This subset has also been revised, and is known to be more consistently annotated. This is the release we use in our experiments. Its key properties, compared with the Penn Treebank, (hereafter PTB) are the following :

Size : The FTB is made of 385 458 tokens and 12351 sentences, that is the third of the PTB. The average length of a sentence is 31 tokens in the FTB, versus 24 tokens in the PTB.

Inflection : French morphology is richer than English and leads to increased data sparseness for statistical parsing. There are 24098 types in the FTB, entailing an average of 16 tokens occurring for each type (versus 12 for the PTB).

Flat structure : The annotation scheme is flatter in the FTB than in the PTB. For instance, there are no VPs for finite verbs, and only one sentential level for sentences whether introduced by complementizer or not. We can measure the corpus flatness using the ratio between tokens and non terminal symbols, excluding preterminals. We obtain 0.69 NT symbol per token for FTB and 1.01 for the PTB.

Compounds : Compounds are explicitly annotated (see the compound *peut-être* in Figure 1) and very frequent : 14,52% of tokens are part of a compound. They include digital numbers (written with spaces in French *10 000*), very frozen compounds *pomme de terre (potato)* but also named entities or sequences whose meaning is compositional but where insertion is rare or difficult (*garde d'enfant (child care)*).

Now let us focus on what is expressed in the French annotation scheme, and why syntactic information is split between constituency and functional annotation.

Syntactic categories and constituents capture distributional generalizations. A syntactic category groups forms that share distributional properties. Nonterminal symbols that label the constituents are a further generalizations over sequences of categories or constituents. For instance about anywhere it is grammatical to have a given NP, it is implicitly assumed that it will also be grammatical - though maybe nonsensical - to have instead any other NPs. Of course this is known to be false in many cases : for instance NPs with or without determiners have very different distributions in French (that may justify a different label) but they also share a lot. Moreover, if words are taken into account, and not just sequences of categories, then constituent labels are a very coarse generalization. Constituents also encode dependencies : for instance the different PP-attachment for the sentences *I ate a cake with cream / with a fork* reflects that *with cream* depends on *cake*, whereas *with a fork* depends on *ate*. More precisely, a syntagmatic tree can be interpreted as a dependency structure using the following conventions :

for each constituent, given the dominating symbol and the internal sequence of symbols, (i) a head symbol can be isolated and (ii) the siblings of that head can be interpreted as containing dependents of that head. Given these constraints, the syntagmatic structure may exhibit various degree of flatness for internal structures.

Functional annotation Dependencies are encoded in constituents. While X-bar inspired constituents are supposed to contain all the syntactic information, in the FTB the shape of the constituents does not necessarily express unambiguously the *type* of dependency existing between a head and a dependent appearing in the same constituent. Yet this is crucial for example to extract the underlying predicate-argument structures. This has led to a "flat" annotation scheme, completed with functional annotations that inform on the type of dependency existing between a verb and its dependents. This was chosen for French to reflect, for instance, the possibility to mix post-verbal modifiers and complements (Figure 2), or to mix post-verbal subject and post-verbal indirect complements : a post verbal NP in the FTB can correspond to a temporal modifier, (most often) a direct object, or an inverted subject, and in the three cases other subcategorized complements may appear.

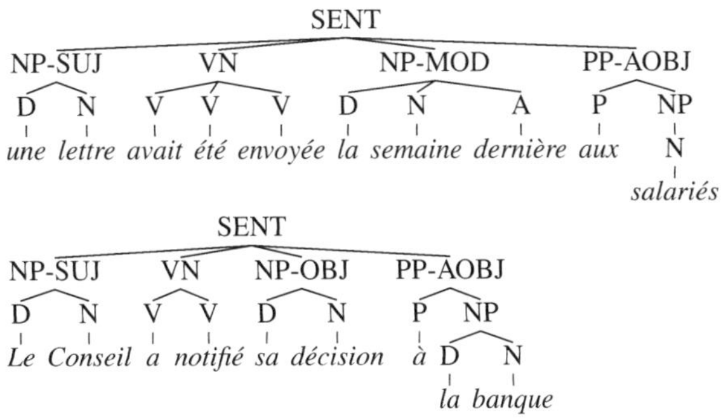

Figure 2: Two examples of post-verbal NPs : a direct object and a temporal modifier

3 Algorithms for probabilistic grammar learning

We propose here to investigate how to apply statistical parsing techniques mainly tested on English, to another language – French –. In this section we briefly introduce the algorithms investigated.

Though Probabilistic Context Free Grammars (PCFG) is a baseline formalism for probabilistic parsing, it suffers a fundamental problem for the purpose of natural language parsing : the independence assumptions made by the model are too strong. In other words all decisions are local to a grammar rule.

However as clearly pointed out by (Johnson, 1998) decisions have to take into account non local grammatical properties: for instance a noun phrase realized in subject position is more likely to be realized by a pronoun than a noun phrase realized in object position. Solving this first methodological issue, has led to solutions dubbed hereafter as *unlexicalized statistical parsing* (Johnson, 1998; Klein and Manning, 2003a; Matsuzaki et al., 2005; Petrov et al., 2006).

A second class of non local decisions to be taken into account while parsing natural languages are related to handling lexical constraints. As shown above the subcategorization properties of a predicative word may have an impact on the decisions concerning the tree structures to be associated to a given sentence. Solving this second methodological issue has led to solutions dubbed hereafter as *lexicalized parsing* (Charniak, 2000; Collins, 1999).

In a supervised setting, a third and practical problem turns out to be critical: that of *data sparseness* since available treebanks are generally too small to get reasonable probability estimates. Three class of solutions are possible to reduce data sparseness: (1) enlarging the data manually or automatically (e.g. (McClosky et al., 2006) uses self-training to perform this step) (2) smoothing, usually this is performed using a markovization procedure (Collins, 1999; Klein and Manning, 2003a) and (3) make the data more coarse (i.e. clustering).

3.1 Lexicalized algorithm

The first algorithm we use is the lexicalized parser of (Collins, 1999). It is called lexicalized, as it annotates non terminal nodes with an additional latent symbol: the head word of the subtree. This additional information attached to the categories aims at capturing bilexical dependencies in order to perform informed attachment choices.

The addition of these numerous latent symbols to non terminals naturally entails an over-specialization of the resulting models. To ensure generalization, it therefore requires to add additional simplifying assumptions formulated as a variant of usual naïve Bayesian-style simplifying assumptions: the probability of emitting a non head node is assumed to depend on the head and the mother node only, and not on other sibling nodes[1].

Since Collins demonstrated his models to significantly improve parsing accuracy over bare PCFG, lexicalization has been thought as a major feature for probabilistic parsing. However two problems are worth stressing here: (1) the reason why these models improve over bare PCFGs is not guaranteed to be tied to the fact that they capture bilexical dependencies and (2) there is no guarantee that capturing non local lexical constraints yields an optimal language model.

Concerning (1) (Gildea, 2001) showed that full lexicalization has indeed small impact on results : he reimplemented an emulation of Collins' Model 1 and found that removing all references to bilexical dependencies in the statistical model[2], resulted in a very small parsing performance decrease (PARSEVAL recall on WSJ decreased from 86.1 to 85.6). Further studies conducted by (Bikel, 2004a) proved indeed that bilexical information were used by the most probable parses. The idea is that most bilexical parameters are very similar to their back-off distribution and have therefore a minor impact. In the case of French, this fact can only be more true, with one third of training data compared to English, and with a much richer inflection that worsens lexical data sparseness.

Concerning (2) the addition of head word annotations is tied to the use of manually defined heuristics highly dependent on the annotation scheme of the PTB. For instance, Collins' models integrate a treatment of coordination that is not adequate for the FTB-like coordination annotation.

3.2 Unlexicalized algorithms

Another class of algorithms arising from (Johnson, 1998; Klein and Manning, 2003a) attempts to attach additional latent symbols to treebank categories without focusing exclusively on lexical head words. For instance the additional annotations will try to capture non local preferences like the fact that an NP in subject position is more likely realized as a pronoun.

The first unlexicalized algorithms set up in this trend (Johnson, 1998; Klein and Manning, 2003a) also use language dependent and manually defined heuristics to add the latent annotations. The specialization induced by this additional annotation is counterbalanced by simplifying assumptions, dubbed markovization (Klein and Manning, 2003a).

Using hand-defined heuristics remains problematic since we have no guarantee that the latent annotations added in this way will allow to extract an optimal language model.

A further development has been first introduced by (Matsuzaki et al., 2005) who recasts the problem of adding latent annotations as an unsupervised learning problem: given an observed PCFG induced from the treebank, the latent grammar is generated by combining every non terminal of the observed grammar to a predefined set H of latent symbols. The parameters of the latent grammar are estimated from the *observed trees* using a specific instantiation of EM.

This first procedure however entails a combinatorial explosion in the size of the latent grammar as $|H|$ increases. (Petrov et al., 2006) (hereafter BKY) overcomes this problem by using the following algorithm: given a PCFG G_0 induced from the treebank, iteratively create n grammars $G_1 \dots G_n$ (with $n = 5$ in practice), where each iterative step is as follows :

- SPLIT Create a new grammar G_i from G_{i-1} by splitting every non terminal of G_i in two new symbols. Estimate G_i's parameters on the observed treebank using a variant of inside-outside. This step adds the latent annotation to the grammar.

- MERGE For each pair of symbols obtained by a previous split, try to merge them back. If the likelihood of the treebank does not get significantly lower (fixed threshold) then keep the symbol merged, otherwise keep the split.

- SMOOTH This step consists in smoothing the probabilities of the grammar rules sharing the same left hand side.

This algorithm yields state-of-the-art results on

[1]This short description cannot do justice to (Collins, 1999) proposal which indeed includes more fine grained informations and a backoff model. We only keep here the key aspects of his work relevant for the current discussion.

[2]Let us consider a dependent constituent C with head word Chw and head tag Cht, and let C be governed by a constituent H, with head word Hhw and head tag Hht. Gildea compares Collins model, where the emission of Chw is conditioned on Hhw, and a "mono-lexical" model, where the emission of Chw is not conditioned on Hhw.

English[3]. Its key interest is that it directly aims at finding an optimal language model without (1) making additional assumptions on the annotation scheme and (2) without relying on hand-defined heuristics. This may be viewed as a case of semi-supervised learning algorithm since the initial supervised learning step is augmented with a second step of unsupervised learning dedicated to assign the latent symbols.

4 Experiments and Results

We investigate how some treebank features impact learning. We describe first the experimental protocol, next we compare results of lexicalized and unlexicalized parsers trained on various "instantiations" of the xml source files of the FTB, and the impact of training set size for both algorithms. Then we focus on studying how words impact the results of the BKYalgorithm.

4.1 Protocol

Treebank setting For all experiments, the treebank is divided into 3 sections : training (80%), development (10%) and test (10%), made of respectively 9881, 1235 and 1235 sentences. We systematically report the results with the compounds merged. Namely, we preprocess the treebank in order to turn each compound into a single token both for training and test.

Software and adaptation to French For the Collins algorithm, we use Bikel's implementation (Bikel, 2004b) (hereafter BIKEL), and we report results using Collins model 1 and model 2, with internal tagging. Adapting model 1 to French requires to design French specific head propagation rules. To this end, we adapted those described by (Dybro-Johansen, 2004) for extracting a Stochastic Tree Adjoining Grammar parser on French. And to adapt model 2, we have further designed French specific argument/adjunct identification rules.

For the BKY approach, we use the Berkeley implementation, with an horizontal markovization h=0, and 5 split/merge cycles. All the required knowledge is contained in the treebank used for training, except for the treatment of unknown or rare words. It clusters unknown words using typographical and morphological information. We adapted these clues to French, following (Arun and Keller, 2005).

Finally we use as a baseline a standard PCFG algorithm, coupled with a trigram tagger (we refer to this setup as TNT/LNCKY algorithm[4]).

Metrics For evaluation, we use the standard PARSEVAL metric of labeled precision/recall, along with unlabeled dependency evaluation, which is known as a more annotation-neutral metric. Unlabeled dependencies are computed using the (Lin, 1995) algorithm, and the Dybro-Johansen's head propagation rules cited above[5]. The unlabeled dependency F-score gives the percentage of input words (excluding punctuation) that receive the correct head.
As usual for probabilistic parsing results, the results are given for sentences of the test set of less than 40 words (which is true for 992 sentences of the test set), and punctuation is ignored for F-score computation with both metrics.

4.2 Comparison using minimal tagsets

We first derive from the FTB a minimally-informed treebank, TREEBANKMIN, instantiated from the xml source by using only the major syntactic categories and no other feature. In each experiment (Table 1) we observe that the BKY algorithm significantly outperforms Collins models, for both metrics.

metric \ parser	BKY	BIKEL M1	BIKEL M2	TNT/ LNCKY
PARSEVAL LP	85.25	78.86	80.68	68.74
PARSEVAL LR	84.46	78.84	80.58	67.93
PARSEVAL F_1	**84.85**	78.85	80.63	68.33
Unlab. dep. Prec.	90.23	85.74	87.60	79.50
Unlab. dep. Rec.	89.95	85.72	86.90	79.37
Unlab. dep. F_1	**90.09**	85.73	87.25	79.44

Table 1: Results for parsers trained on FTB with minimal tagset

[3](Petrov et al., 2006) obtain an F-score=90.1 for sentences of less than 40 words.

[4]The tagger is TNT (Brants, 2000), and the parser is LNCKY, that is distributed by Mark Johnson (http://www.cog.brown.edu/~mj/Software.htm). Formally because of the tagger, this is not a strict PCFG setup. Rather, it gives a practical trade-off, in which the tagger includes the lexical smoothing for unknown and rare words.

[5]For this evaluation, the gold constituent trees are converted into pseudo-gold dependency trees (that may contain errors). Then parsed constituent trees are converted into parsed dependency trees, that are matched against the pseudo-gold trees.

4.3 Impact of training data size

How do the unlexicalized and lexicalized approaches perform with respect to size? We compare in figure 3 the parsing performance BKY and COLLINSM1, on increasingly large subsets of the FTB, in perfect tagging mode[6] and using a more detailed tagset (CC tagset, described in the next experiment). The same 1235-sentences test set is used for all subsets, and the development set's size varies along with the training set's size. BKY outperforms the lexicalized model even with small amount of data (around 3000 training sentences). Further, the parsing improvement that would result from more training data seems higher for BKY than for Bikel.

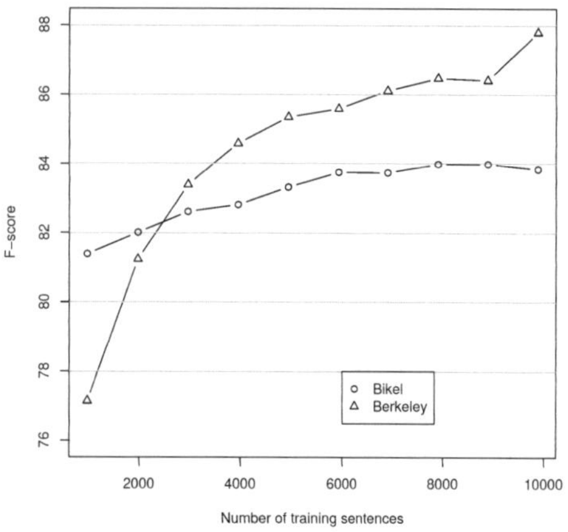

Figure 3: Parsing Learning curve on FTB with CC-tagset, in perfect-tagging

This potential increase for BKY results if we had more French annotated data is somehow confirmed by the higher results reported for BKY training on the Penn Treebank (Petrov et al., 2006) : F_1=90.2. We can show though that the 4 points increase when training on English data is not only due to size : we extracted from the Penn Treebank a subset comparable to the FTB, with respect to number of tokens and average length of sentences. We obtain F_1=88.61 with BKY training.

4.4 Symbol refinements

It is well-known that certain treebank transformations involving symbol refinements improve PCFGs (see for instance parent-transformation of (Johnson, 1998), or various symbol refinements in (Klein and Manning., 2003b)). Lexicalization itself can be seen as symbol refinements (with backoff though). For BKY, though the key point is to automatize symbol splits, it is interesting to study whether manual splits still help.

We have thus experimented BKY training with various tagsets. The FTB contains rich morphological information, that can be used to split preterminal symbols : main coarse category (there are 13), subcategory (`subcat` feature refining the main cat), and inflectional information (`mph` feature).

We report in Table 2 results for the four tagsets, where terminals are made of : MIN: main cat, SUBCAT: main cat + subcat feature, MAX: cat + subcat + all inflectional information, CC: cat + verbal mood + wh feature.

Tagset	Nb of tags	Parseval F_1	Unlab. dep F_1	Tagging Acc
MIN	13	84.85	90.09	97.35
SUBCAT	34	85.74	–	96.63
MAX	250	84.13	–	92.20
CC	28	**86.41**	**90.99**	96.83

Table 2: Tagset impact on learning with BKY (own tagging)

The corpus instantiation with CC tagset is our best trade-off between tagset informativeness and obtained parsing performance[7]. It is also the best result obtained for French probabilistic parsing. This demonstrates though that the BKY learning is not optimal since manual a priori symbol refinements significantly impact the results.

We also tried to learn structures with functional annotation attached to the labels : we obtain PARSEVAL F_1=78.73 with tags from the CC tagset + grammatical function. This degradation, due to data sparseness and/or non local constraints badly captured by the model, currently constrains us to use a language model without functional informations. As stressed in the introduction, this limits the interpretability of the parses and it is a trade-off between generalization and interpretability.

4.5 Lexicon and Inflection impact

French has a rich morphology that allows some degree of word order variation, with respect to

[6]For BKY, we simulate perfect tagging by changing words into word+tag in training, dev and test sets. We obtain around 99.8 tagging accuracy, errors are due to unknown words.

[7]The differences are statistically significant : using a standard t-test, we obtain p-value=0.015 between MIN and SUBCAT, and p-value=0.002 between CC and SUBCAT.

English. For probabilistic parsing, this can have contradictory effects : (i) on the one hand, this induces more data sparseness : the occurrences of a French regular verb are potentially split into more than 60 forms, versus 5 for an English verb; (ii) on the other hand, inflection encodes agreements, that can serve as clues for syntactic attachments.

Experiment In order to measure the impact of inflection, we have tested to cluster word forms on a morphological basis, namely to partly cancel inflection. Using lemmas as word form classes seems too coarse : it would not allow to distinguish for instance between a finite verb and a participle, though they exhibit different distributional properties. Instead we use as word form classes, the couple lemma + syntactic category. For example for verbs, given the CC tagset, this amounts to keeping 6 different forms (for the 6 moods).
To test this grouping, we derive a treebank where words are replaced by the concatenation of lemma + category for training and testing the parser. Since it entails a perfect tagging, it has to be compared to results in perfect tagging mode : more precisely, we simulate perfect tagging by replacing word forms by the concatenation form+tag.
Moreover, it is tempting to study the impact of a more drastic clustering of word forms : that of using the sole syntactic category to group word forms (we replace each word by its tag). This amounts to test a pure unlexicalized learning.

Discussion Results are shown in Figure 4. We make three observations : First, comparing the terminal=tag curves with the other two, it appears that the parser does take advantage of lexical information to rank parses, even for this "unlexicalized" algorithm. Yet the relatively small increase clearly shows that lexical information remains underused, probably because of lexical data sparseness.
Further, comparing terminal=lemma+tag and terminal=form+tag curves, we observe that grouping words into lemmas helps reducing this sparseness. And third, the lexicon impact evolution (i.e. the increment between terminal=tag and terminal=form+tag curves) is stable, once the training size is superior to approx. 3000 sentences[8]. This suggests that only very frequent words matter, otherwise words' impact should be more and more important as training material augments.

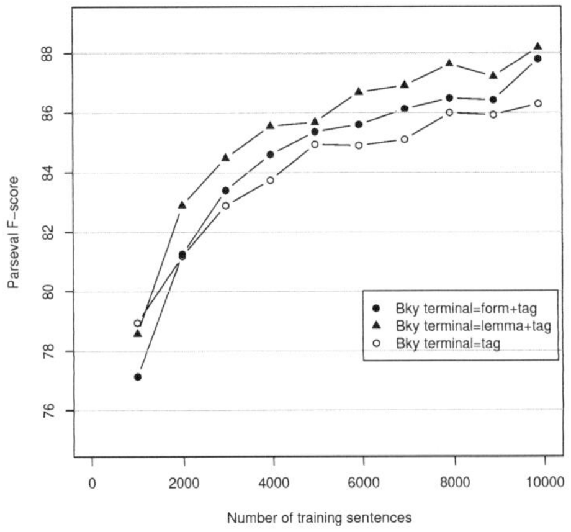

Figure 4: Impact of clustering word forms (training on FTB with CC-tagset, in perfect-tagging)

5 Related Work

Previous works on French probabilistic parsing are those of (Arun and Keller, 2005), (Schluter and van Genabith, 2007), (Schluter and van Genabith, 2008). One major difficulty for comparison is that all three works use a different version of the training corpus. Arun reports results on probabilistic parsing, using an older version of the FTB and using lexicalized models (Collins M1 and M2 models, and the bigram model). It is difficult to compare our results with Arun's work, since the treebank he has used is obsolete (FTB-V0). He obtains for Model 1 : LR=80.35 / LP=79.99, and for the bigram model : LR=81.15 / LP=80.84, with minimal tagset and internal tagging. The results with FTB (revised subset of FTB-V0) with minimal

[8] This is true for all points in the curves, except for the last step, i.e. when full training set is used. We performed a 10-fold cross validation to limit sample effects. For the BKYtraining with CC tagset, and own tagging, we obtain an average F-score of 85.44 (with a rather high standard deviation σ=1.14). For the clustering word forms experiment, using the full training set, we obtain : 86.64 for terminal=form+tag (σ=1.15), 87.33 for terminal=lemma+tag (σ=0.43), and 85.72 for terminal=tag (σ=0.43). Hence our conclusions (words help even with unlexicalized algorithm, and further grouping words into lemmas helps) hold independently of sampling.

tagset (Table 1) are comparable for COLLINSM1, and nearly 5 points higher for BKY.

It is also interesting to review (Arun and Keller, 2005) conclusion, built on a comparison with the German situation : at that time lexicalization was thought (Dubey and Keller, 2003) to have no sizable improvement on German parsing, trained on the Negra treebank, that uses a flat structures. So (Arun and Keller, 2005) conclude that since lexicalization helps much more for parsing French, with a flat annotation, then word-order flexibility is the key-factor that makes lexicalization useful (if word order is fixed, cf. French and English) and useless (if word order is flexible, cf. German). This conclusion does not hold today. First, it can be noted that as far as word order flexibility is concerned, French stands in between English and German. Second, it has been proven that lexicalization helps German probabilistic parsing (Kübler et al., 2006). Finally, these authors show that markovization of the unlexicalized Stanford parser gives almost the same increase in performance than lexicalization, both for the Negra treebank and the Tüba-D/Z treebank. This conclusion is reinforced by the results we have obtained : the unlexicalized, markovized, PCFG-LA algorithm outperforms the Collins' lexicalized model.

(Schluter and van Genabith, 2007) aim at learning LFG structures for French. To do so, and in order to learn first a Collins parser, N. Schluter created a modified treebank, the MFT, in order (i) to fit her underlying theoretical requirements, (ii) to increase the treebank coherence by error mining and (iii) to improve the performance of the learnt parser. The MFT contains 4739 sentences taken from the FTB, with semi-automatic transformations. These include increased rule stratification, symbol refinements (for information propagation), coordination raising with some manual re-annotation, and the addition of functional tags. MFT has also undergone a phase of error mining, using the (Dickinson and Meurers, 2005) software, and following manual correction. She reports a 79.95% F-score on a 400 sentence test set, which compares almost equally with Arun's results on the original 20000 sentence treebank. So she attributes her results to the increased coherence of her smaller treebank. Indeed, we ran the BKY training on the MFT, and we get F-score=84.31. While this is less in absolute than the BKY results obtained with FTB (cf. results in table 2), it is indeed very high if training data size is taken into account (cf. the BKY learning curve in figure 3). This good result raises the open question of identifying which modifications in the MFT (error mining and correction, tree transformation, symbol refinements) have the major impact.

6 Conclusion

This paper reports results in statistical parsing for French with both unlexicalized (Petrov et al., 2006) and lexicalized parsers. To our knowledge, both results are state of the art on French for each paradigm.

Both algorithms try to overcome PCFG's simplifying assumptions by some specialization of the grammatical labels. For the lexicalized approach, the annotation of symbols with lexical head is known to be rarely fully used in practice (Gildea, 2001), what is really used being the category of the lexical head.

We observe that the second approach (BKY) constantly outperforms the lexicalist strategy *à la* (Collins, 1999). We observe however that (Petrov et al., 2006)'s semi-supervised learning procedure is not fully optimal since a manual refinement of the treebank labelling turns out to improve the parsing results.

Finally we observe that the semi-supervised BKY algorithm does take advantage of lexical information : removing words degrades results. The preterminal symbol splits percolates lexical distinctions. Further, grouping words into lemmas helps for a morphologically rich language such as French. So, an intermediate clustering standing between syntactic category and lemma is thought to yield better results in the future.

7 Acknowledgments

We thank N. Schluter and J. van Genabith for kindly letting us run BKY on the MFT, and A. Arun for answering our questions. We also thank the reviewers for valuable comments and references. The work of the second author was partly funded by the "Prix Diderot Innovation 2007", from University Paris 7.

References

Anne Abeillé, Lionel Clément, and Alexandra Kinyon. 2000. Building a treebank for french. In *Proceedings of the 2nd International Conference Language Resources and Evaluation (LREC'00)*.

Anne Abeillé, Lionel Clément, and François Toussenel, 2003. *Building a treebank for French*. Kluwer, Dordrecht.

Abhishek Arun and Frank Keller. 2005. Lexicalization in crosslinguistic probabilistic parsing: The case of french. In *Proceedings of the 43rd Annual Meeting of the Association for Computational Linguistics*, pages 306–313, Ann Arbor, MI.

Daniel M. Bikel. 2004a. A distributional analysis of a lexicalized statistical parsing model. In *Proc. of Empirical Methods in Natural Language Processing (EMNLP 2004)*, volume 4, pages 182–189, Barcelona, Spain.

Daniel M. Bikel. 2004b. Intricacies of Collins' Parsing Model. *Computational Linguistics*, 30(4):479–511.

Thorsten Brants. 2000. Tnt – a statistical part-of-speech tagger. In *Proceedings of the 6th Applied NLP Conference (ANLP)*, Seattle-WA.

Eugene Charniak. 2000. A maximum-entropy-inspired parser. In *Proceedings of the Annual Meeting of the North American Association for Computational Linguistics (NAACL-00)*, pages 132–139, Seattle, Washington.

Michael Collins. 1999. *Head driven statistical models for natural language parsing*. Ph.D. thesis, University of Pennsylvania, Philadelphia.

Benoit Crabbé and Marie Candito. 2008. Expériences d'analyse syntaxique statistique du français. In *Actes de la 15ème Conférence sur le Traitement Automatique des Langues Naturelles (TALN'08)*, pages 45–54, Avignon.

Markus Dickinson and W. Detmar Meurers. 2005. Prune diseased branches to get healthy trees! how to find erroneous local trees in treebank and why it matters. In *Proceedings of the 4th Workshop on Treebanks and Linguistic Theories (TLT 2005)*, Barcelona, Spain.

Amit Dubey and Frank Keller. 2003. Probabilistic parsing for german using sister-head dependencies. In *In Proceedings of the 41st Annual Meeting of the Association for Computational Linguistics*, pages 96–103.

Ane Dybro-Johansen. 2004. Extraction automatique de grammaires á partir d'un corpus français. Master's thesis, Université Paris 7.

Daniel Gildea. 2001. Corpus variation and parser performance. In *Proceedings of the First Conference on Empirical Methods in Natural Language Processing (EMNLP)*, pages 167–202.

Mark Johnson. 1998. PCFG models of linguistic tree representations. *Computational Linguistics*, 24(4):613–632.

Dan Klein and Christopher D. Manning. 2003a. Accurate unlexicalized parsing. In *Proceedings of the 41st Annual Meeting on Association for Computational Linguistics-Volume 1*, pages 423–430. Association for Computational Linguistics Morristown, NJ, USA.

Dan Klein and Christopher D. Manning. 2003b. Accurate unlexicalized parsing. In *Proceedings of the 41st Meeting of the Association for Computational Linguistics*.

Sandra Kübler, Erhard W. Hinrichs, and Wolfgang Maier. 2006. Is it really that difficult to parse german? In *Proceedings of the 2006 Conference on Empirical Methods in Natural Language Processing*, pages 111–119, Sydney, Australia, July. Association for Computational Linguistics.

Dekang Lin. 1995. A dependency-based method for evaluating broad-coverage parsers. In *International Joint Conference on Artificial Intelligence*, pages 1420–1425, Montreal.

Takuya Matsuzaki, Yusuke Miyao, and Jun'ichi Tsujii. 2005. Probabilistic cfg with latent annotations. In *Proceedings of the 43rd Annual Meeting of the Association for Computational Linguistics (ACL)*, pages 75–82.

David McClosky, Eugene Charniak, and Mark Johnson. 2006. Effective self-training for parsing. In *Proceedings of the Human Language Technology Conference of the NAACL, Main Conference*, pages 152–159, New York City, USA, June. Association for Computational Linguistics.

Slav Petrov, Leon Barrett, Romain Thibaux, and Dan Klein. 2006. Learning accurate, compact, and interpretable tree annotation. In *Proceedings of the 21st International Conference on Computational Linguistics and 44th Annual Meeting of the Association for Computational Linguistics*, Sydney, Australia, July. Association for Computational Linguistics.

Natalie Schluter and Josef van Genabith. 2007. Preparing, restructuring, and augmenting a french treebank: Lexicalised parsers or coherent treebanks? In *Proceedings of PACLING 07*.

Natalie Schluter and Josef van Genabith. 2008. Treebank-based acquisition of lfg parsing resources for french. In European Language Resources Association (ELRA), editor, *Proceedings of the Sixth International Language Resources and Evaluation (LREC'08)*, Marrakech, Morocco, may.

Upper Bounds for Unsupervised Parsing with Unambiguous Non-Terminally Separated Grammars

Franco M. Luque and **Gabriel Infante-Lopez**
Grupo de Procesamiento de Lenguaje Natural
Universidad Nacional de Córdoba & CONICET
Argentina
`{francolq|gabriel}@famaf.unc.edu.ar`

Abstract

Unambiguous Non-Terminally Separated (UNTS) grammars have properties that make them attractive for grammatical inference. However, these properties do not state the maximal performance they can achieve when they are evaluated against a gold treebank that is not produced by an UNTS grammar. In this paper we investigate such an upper bound. We develop a method to find an upper bound for the unlabeled $F1$ performance that any UNTS grammar can achieve over a given treebank. Our strategy is to characterize all possible versions of the gold treebank that UNTS grammars can produce and to find the one that optimizes a metric we define. We show a way to translate this score into an upper bound for the $F1$. In particular, we show that the $F1$ parsing score of any UNTS grammar can not be beyond 82.2% when the gold treebank is the WSJ10 corpus.

1 Introduction

Unsupervised learning of natural language has received a lot of attention in the last years, e.g., Klein and Manning (2004), Bod (2006a) and Seginer (2007). Most of them use sentences from a treebank for training and trees from the same treebank for evaluation. As such, the best model for unsupervised parsing is the one that reports the best performance.

Unambiguous Non-Terminally Separated (UNTS) grammars have properties that make them attractive for grammatical inference. These grammars have been shown to be PAC-learnable in polynomial time (Clark, 2006), meaning that under certain circumstances, the underlying grammar can be learned from a sample of the underlying language. Moreover, UNTS grammars have been successfully used to induce grammars from unannotated corpora in competitions of learnability of formal languages (Clark, 2007).

UNTS grammars can be used for modeling natural language. They can be induced using any training material, the induced models can be evaluated using trees from a treebank, and their performance can be compared against state-of-the-art unsupervised models. Different learning algorithms might produce different grammars and, consequently, different scores. The fact that the class of UNTS grammars is PAC learnable does not convey any information on the possible scores that different UNTS grammars might produce. From a performance oriented perspective it might be possible to have an upper bound over the set of possible scores of UNTS grammars. Knowing an upper bound is complementary to knowing that the class of UNTS grammars is PAC learnable.

Such upper bound has to be defined specifically for UNTS grammars and has to take into account the treebank used as test set. The key question is how to compute it. Suppose that we want to evaluate the performance of a given UNTS grammar using a treebank. The candidate grammar produces a tree for each sentence and those trees are compared to the original treebank. We can think that the candidate grammar has produced a new version of the treebank, and that the score of the grammar is a measure of the closeness of the new treebank to the original treebank. Finding the best upper bound is equivalent to finding the closest UNTS version of the treebank to the original one.

Such bounds are difficult to find for most classes of languages because the search space is the set of all possible versions of the treebank that might have been produced by any grammar in the class under study. In order to make the problem tractable, we need the formalism to have an easy way to characterize all the versions of a treebank

Proceedings of the EACL 2009 Workshop on Computational Linguistic Aspects of Grammatical Inference, pages 58–65,
Athens, Greece, 30 March 2009.

it might produce. UNTS grammars have a special characterization that makes the search space easy to define but whose exploration is NP-hard.

In this paper we present a way to characterize UNTS grammars and a metric function to measure the closeness between two different version of a treebank. We show that the problem of finding the closest UNTS version of the treebank can be described as Maximum Weight Independent Set (MWIS) problem, a well known NP-hard problem (Karp, 1972). The exploration algorithm returns a version of the treebank that is the closest to the gold standard in terms of our own metric.

We show that the $F1$-measure is related to our measure and that it is possible to find and upper bound of the $F1$-performance for all UNTS grammars. Moreover, we compute this upper bound for the WSJ10, a subset of the Penn Treebank (Marcus et al., 1994) using POS tags as the alphabet. The upper bound we found is 82.2% for the $F1$ measure. Our result suggest that UNTS grammars are a formalism that has the potential to achieve state-of-the-art unsupervised parsing performance but does not guarantee that there exists a grammar that can actually achieve the 82.2%.

To the best of our knowledge, there is no previous research on finding upper bounds for performance over a concrete class of grammars. In Klein and Manning (2004), the authors compute an upper bound for parsing with binary trees a gold treebank that is not binary. This upper bound, that is 88.1% for the WSJ10, is for any parser that returns binary trees, including the concrete models developed in the same work. But their upper bound does not use any specific information of the concrete models that may help them to find better ones.

The rest of the paper is organized as follows. Section 2 presents our characterization of UNTS grammars. Section 3 introduces the metric we optimized and explains how the closest version of the treebank is found. Section 4 explains how the upper bound for our metric is translated to an upper bound of the $F1$ score. Section 5 presents our bound for UNTS grammars using the WSJ10 and finally Section 6 concludes the paper.

2 UNTS Grammars and Languages

Formally, a context free grammar $G = (\Sigma, N, S, P)$ is said to be Non-Terminally Separated (NTS) if, for all $X, Y \in N$ and $\alpha, \beta, \gamma \in (\Sigma \cup N)^*$ such that $X \stackrel{*}{\Rightarrow} \alpha\beta\gamma$ and $Y \stackrel{*}{\Rightarrow} \beta$, we have that $X \stackrel{*}{\Rightarrow} \alpha Y \gamma$ (Clark, 2007). Unambiguous NTS (UNTS) grammars are those NTS grammars that parses unambiguously every instance of the language.

Given any grammar G, a substring s of $r \in L(G)$ is called a *constituent* of r if and only if there is an X in N such that $S \stackrel{*}{\Rightarrow} uXv \stackrel{*}{\Rightarrow} usv = r$. In contrast, a string s is called a non-constituent or *distituent* of $r \in L(G)$ if s is not a constituent of r. We say that s is a constituent of a language $L(G)$ if for every r that contains s, s is a constituent of r. In contrast, s is a distituent of $L(G)$ if for every r where s occurs, s is a distituent of r.

An interesting characterization of finite UNTS grammars is that every substring that appear in some string of the language is always a constituent or always a distituent. In other words, if there is a string r in $L(G)$ for which s is a constituent, then s is a constituent of $L(G)$. By means of this property, if we ignore the non-terminal labels, a finite UNTS language is fully determined by its set of constituents C. We can show this property for finite UNTS languages. We believe that it can also be shown for non-finite cases, but for our purposes the finite cases suffices, because we use grammars to parse finite sets of sentences, specifically, the sentences of test treebanks. We know that for every finite subset of an infinite language produced by a UNTS grammar G, there is a UNTS grammar G' whose language is finite and that parses the finite subset as G. If we look for the upper bound among the grammars that produce a finite language, this upper bound is also an upper bound for the class of infinite UNTS grammars.

The UNTS characterization plays a very important role in the way we look for the upper bound. Our method focuses on how to determine which of the constituents that appear in the gold are actually the constituents that produce the upper bound. Suppose that a given gold treebank contains two strings α and β such that they *occur overlapped*. That is, there exist non-empty strings α', γ, β' such that $\alpha = \alpha'\gamma$ and $\beta = \gamma\beta'$ and $\alpha'\gamma\beta'$ occurs in the treebank. If C is the set of constituents of a UNTS grammar it can not have both α and β. It might have one or the other, but if both belong to C the resulting language can not be UNTS. In order to find the closest UNTS grammar we design a procedure that looks for the subset of all substrings that occur in the sentences of the gold treebank that can be the constituent set C

of a grammar. We do not explicitly build a UNTS grammar, but find the set C that produces the best score.

We say that two strings α and β are *compatible* in a language L if they do not occur overlapped in L, and hence they both can be members of C. If we think of L as a subset of an infinite language, it is not possible to check that two overlapping strings do not appear overlapped in the "real" language and hence that they are actually compatible. Nevertheless, we can guarantee compatibility between two strings α, β by requiring that they do not overlap at all, this is, that there are no non-empty strings α', γ, β' such that $\alpha = \alpha'\gamma$ and $\beta = \gamma\beta'$. We call this type of compatibility *strong compatibility*. Strong compatibility ensures that two strings can belong to C regardless of L. In our experiments we focus on finding the best set C of compatible strings.

Any set of compatible strings C extracted from the gold treebank can be used to produce a new version of the treebank. For example, Figure 1 shows two trees from the WSJ Penn Treebank. The string "in the dark" occurs as a constituent in (a) and as a distituent in (b). If C contains "in the dark", it can not contain "the dark clouds" given that they overlap in the yield of (b). As a consequence, the new treebank correctly contains the subtree in (a) but not the one in (b). Instead, the yield of (b) is described as in (c) in the new treebank.

C defines a new version of the treebank that satisfies the UNTS property. Our goal is to obtain a treebank T' such that (a) T' and T are treebanks over the same set of sentences, (b) T' is UNTS, and (c) T' is the closest treebank to T in terms of performance. The three of them imply that any other UNTS grammar is not as similar as the one we found.

3 Finding the Best UNTS Grammar

As our goal is to find the closest grammar in terms of performance, we need to define first a weight for each possible grammar and second, an algorithm that searches for the grammar with the best weight. Ideally, the weight of a candidate grammar should be in terms of $F1$, but we can show that optimization of this particular metric is computationally hard. Instead of defining $F1$ as their score, we introduce a new metric that is easier to optimize, we find the best grammar for this metric, and we show that the possible values of $F1$ can be bounded by a function that takes this score as argument. In this section we present our metric and the technique we use to find a grammar that reports the best value for our metric.

If the original treebank T is not produced by any UNTS grammar, then there are strings in T that are constituents in some sentences and that are distituents in some other sentences. For each one of them we need a procedure to decide whether they are members of C or not. If a string α appears a significant number of times more as a constituent than as a distituent the procedure may choose to include it in C at the price of being wrong a few times. That is, the new version of T has all occurrences of α either as constituents or as distituents. The treebank that has all of its occurrences as constituents differs from the original in that there are some occurrences of α that were originally distituents and are marked as constituents. Similarly, if α is marked as distituent in the new treebank, it has occurrences of α that were constituents in T.

The decision procedure becomes harder when all the substrings that appear in the treebank are considered. The increase in complexity is a consequence of the number of decisions the procedure needs to take and the way these decisions interfere one with another. We show that the problem of determining the set C is naturally embedded in a graph NP-hard problem. We define a way to look for the optimal grammars by translating our problem to a well known graph problem. Let L be the the set of sentences in a treebank, and let $S(L)$ be all the possible non-empty proper substrings of L. We build a weighted undirected graph G in terms of the treebank as follows. Nodes in G correspond to strings in $S(L)$. The weight of a node is a function $w(s)$ that models our interest of having s selected as a constituent; $w(s)$ is defined in terms of some information derived from the gold treebank T and we discuss it later in this section. Finally, two nodes a and b are connected by an edge if their two corresponding strings conflict in a sentence of T (i.e., they are not compatible in L).

Not all elements of L are in $S(L)$. We did not include L in $S(L)$ for two practical reasons. The first one is that to require L in $S(L)$ is too restrictive. It states that all strings in L are in fact constituents. If two string ab and bc of L occur overlapped in a third string abc then there is no UNTS grammar capable of having the three of

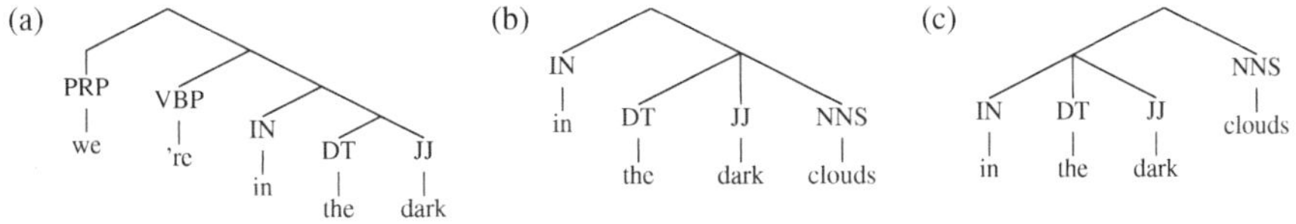

Figure 1: (a) and (b) are two subtrees that show "in the dark" as a constituent and as a distituent respectively. (c) shows the result of choosing "in the dark" as a constituent.

them as constituents. The second one is that including them produces graphs that are too sparse. If they are included in the graph, we know that any solution should contain them, consequently, all their neighbors do not belong to any solution and they can be removed from the graph. Our experiments show that the graph that results from removing nodes related to nodes representing strings in L are too small to produce any interesting result.

By means of representing the treebank as a graph, selecting a set of constituents $C \subseteq S(L)$ is equivalent to selecting an independent set of nodes in the graph. An *independent set* is a subset of the set of nodes that do not have any pair of nodes connected by an edge. Clearly, there are exponentially many possible ways to select an independent set, and each of these sets represents a set of constituents. But, since we are interested in the best set of constituents, we associate to each independent set C the weight $W(C)$ defined as $\sum_{s \in C} w(s)$. Our aim is then to find a set C_{max} that maximizes this weight. This problem is a well known problem of graph theory known in the literature as the Maximum Weight Independent Set (MWIS) problem. This problem is also known to be NP-hard (Karp, 1972).

We still have to choose a definition for $w(s)$. We want to find the grammar that maximizes $F1$. Unfortunately, $F1$ can not be expressed in terms of a sum of weights. Maximization of $F1$ is beyond the expressiveness of our model, but our strategy is to define a measure that correlates with $F1$ and that can be expressed as a sum of weights.

In order to introduce our measure, we first define $c(s)$ and $d(s)$ as the number of times a string s appears in the gold treebank T as a constituent and as a distituent respectively. Observe that if we choose to include s as a constituent of C, the resulting treebank T' contains all the $c(s) + d(s)$ occurrences of s as a constituent. $c(s)$ of the s occurrences in T' are constituents as they are in T and $d(s)$ of the occurrences are constituents in T' but are in fact distituents in T. We want to maximize $c(s)$ and minimize $d(s)$ at the same time. This can be done by defining the contribution of a string s to the overall score as

$$w(s) = c(s) - d(s).$$

With this definition of w, the weight $W(C) = \sum_{s \in C} w(s)$ becomes the number of constituents of T' that are in T minus the number of constituents that do not. If we define the number of *hits* to be $H(C) = \sum_{s \in C} c(s)$ and the number of *misses* to be $M(C) = \sum_{s \in C} d(s)$ we have that

$$W(C) = H(C) - M(C). \quad (1)$$

As we confirm in Section 5, graphs tend to be very big. In order to reduce the size of the graphs, if a string s has $w(s) \leq 0$, we do not include its corresponding node in the graph. An independent set that does not include s has an equal or higher W than the same set including s.

For example, let T be the treebank in Figure 2 (a). The sets of substrings such that $w(c) \geq 0$ is $\{da, cd, bc, cda, ab, bch\}$. The graph that corresponds to this set of strings is given in Figure 3. Nodes corresponding to strings $\{dabch, bcda, abe, abf, abg, bci, daj\}$ are not shown in the figure because the strings do not belong to $S(L)$. The figure also shows the weights associated to the substrings according to their counts in Figure 2 (a). The shadowed nodes correspond to the independent set that maximizes W. The trees in the Figure 2 (b) are the sentences of the treebank parsed according the optimal independent set.

4 An Upper Bound for F1

Even though finding the independent set that maximizes W is an NP-Hard problem, there are instances where it can be effectively computed, as we show in the next section. The set C_{max} maximizes W for the WSJ10 and we know that all others C produces a lower value of W. In other words, the set C_{max} produce a treebank T_{max} that

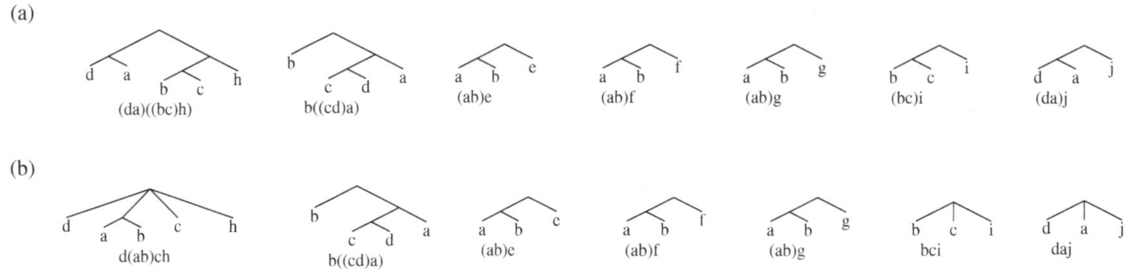

Figure 2: (a) A gold treebank. (b) The treebank generated by the grammar $C = L \cup \{cd, ab, cda\}$.

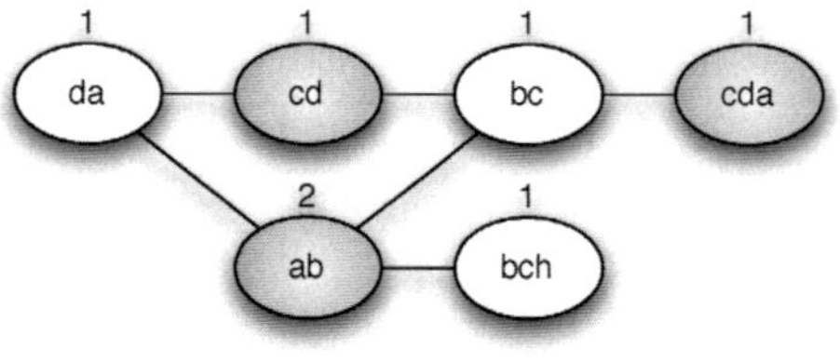

Figure 3: Graph for the treebank of Figure 2.

is the closest UNTS version to the WSJ10 in terms of W. We can compute the precision, recall and $F1$ for C_{max} but there is no warranty that the $F1$ score is the best for all the UNTS grammars. This is the case because $F1$ and W do not define the same ordering over the family of candidate constituent sets C: there are gold treebanks T (used for computing the metrics), and sets C_1, C_2 such that $F1(C_1) < F1(C_2)$ and $W(C_1) > W(C_2)$. For example, consider the gold treebank T in Figure 4 (a). The table in Figure 4 (b) displays two sets C_1 and C_2, the treebanks they produce, and their values of $F1$ and W. Note that C_2 is the result of adding the string ef to C_1, also note that $c(ef) = 1$ and $d(ef) = 2$. This improves the $F1$ score but produces a lower W.

The $F1$ measure we work with is the one defined in the recent literature of unsupervised parsing (Klein and Manning, 2004). $F1$ is defined in terms of Precision and Recall as usual, and the last two measures are micro-averaged measures that include full-span brackets, and that ignore both unary branches and brackets of span one. For simplicity, the previous example does not count the full-span brackets.

As the example shows, the upper bound for W might not be an upper bound of $F1$, but it is possible to find a way to define an upper bound of $F1$ using the upper bound of W. In this section we define a function f with the following property. Let X and Y be the sets of W-weights and $F1$-weights for all possible UNTS grammars respectively. Then, if w is an upper bound of X, then $f(w)$ is an upper bound of Y. The function f is defined as follows:

$$f(w) = F1\left(\frac{1}{2 - \frac{w}{K}}, 1\right) \tag{2}$$

where $F1(p, r) = \frac{2pr}{p+r}$, and $K = \sum_{s \in S_T} c(s)$ is the total number of constituents in the gold treebank T. From it, we can also derive values for precision and recall: precision $\frac{1}{2-\frac{w}{K}}$ and recall 1. A recall of 1 is clearly an upper bound for all the possible values of recall, but the value given for precision is not necessarily an upper bound for all the possible values of precision. It might exist a grammar having a higher value of precision but whose $F1$ has to be below our upper bound.

The rest of section shows that $f(W)$ is an upper bound for $F1$, the reader not interested in the technicalities can skip it.

The key insight for the proof is that both metrics $F1$ and W can be written in terms of precision and recall. Let T be the treebank that is used to compute all the metrics. And let T' be the treebank produced by a given constituent set C. If a string s belongs to C, then its $c(s) + d(s)$ occurrences in T' are marked as constituents. Moreover, s is correctly tagged a $c(s)$ number of times while it is incorrectly tagged a $d(s)$ number of times. Using this, P, R and $F1$ can be computed for C as follows:

$$\begin{aligned} P(C) &= \frac{\sum_{s \in C} c(s)}{\sum_{s \in C} c(s)+d(s)} \\ &= \frac{H(C)}{H(C)+M(C)} \end{aligned} \tag{3}$$

$$\begin{aligned} R(C) &= \frac{\sum_{s \in C} c(s)}{K} \\ &= \frac{H(C)}{K} \end{aligned} \tag{4}$$

$$\begin{aligned} F1(C) &= \frac{2P(C)R(C)}{P(C)+R(C)} \\ &= \frac{2H(C)}{K+H(C)+M(C)} \end{aligned}$$

(a)

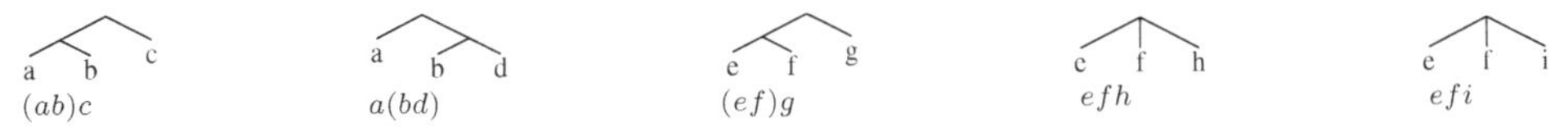

(b)

C	T'_C	P	R	$F1$	W
$C_1 = \{abc, abd, efg, efh, efi, ab\}$	$\{(ab)c, (ab)d, efg, efh, efi\}$	50%	33%	40%	$1 - 1 = 0$
$C_2 = \{abc, abd, efg, efh, efi, ab, ef\}$	$\{(ab)c, (ab)d, (ef)g, (ef)h, (ef)i\}$	40%	67%	50%	$2 - 3 = -1$

Figure 4: (a) A gold treebank. (b) Two grammars, the treebanks they generate, and their scores.

W can also be written in terms of P and R as

$$W(C) = (2 - \frac{1}{P(C)})R(C)K \tag{5}$$

This formula is proved to be equivalent to Equation (1) by replacing $P(C)$ and $R(C)$ with equations (3) and (4) respectively. Using the last two equations, we can rewrite $F1$ and W taking p and r, representing values of precision and recall, as parameters:

$$F1(p, r) = \frac{2pr}{p + r}$$
$$W(p, r) = (2 - \frac{1}{p})rK \tag{6}$$

Using these equations, we can prove that f correctly translates upper bounds of W to upper bounds of $F1$ using calculus. In contrast to $F1$, W not necessarily take values between 0 and 1. Instead, it takes values between K and $-\infty$. Moreover, it is negative when $p < \frac{1}{2}$, and goes to $-\infty$ when p goes to 0. Let C be an arbitrary UNTS grammar, and let p_C, r_C and w_C be its precision, recall and W-weight respectively. Let w be our upper bound, so that $w_C \leq w$. If $f1_C$ is defined as $F1(p_C, r_C)$ we need to show that $f1_C \leq f(w)$. We bound $f1_C$ in two steps. First, we show that

$$f1_C \leq f(w_C)$$

and second, we show that

$$f(w_C) \leq f(w).$$

The first inequality is proved by observing that $f1_C$ and $f(w_C)$ are the values of the function

$$f1(r) = F1\left(\frac{1}{2 - \frac{w_C}{Kr}}, r\right)$$

at the points $r = r_C$ and $r = 1$ respectively. This function corresponds to the line defined by the $F1$ values of all possible models that have a fixed weight $W = w_C$. The function is monotonically increasing in r, so we can apply it to both sides of the following inequality $r_C \leq 1$, which is trivially true. As result, we get $f1_C \leq f(w_C)$ as required. The second inequality is proved by observing that $f(w)$ is monotonically increasing in w, and by applying it to both sides of the hypothesis $w_c \leq w$.

5 UNTS Bounds for the WSJ10 Treebank

In this section we focus on trying to find real upper bounds building the graph for a particular treebank T. We find the best independent set, we build the UNTS version T_{max} of T and we compute the upper bound for $F1$. The treebank we use for experiments is the WSJ10, which consists of the sentences of the WSJ Penn Treebank whose length is at most 10 words after removing punctuation marks (Klein and Manning, 2004). We also removed lexical entries transforming POS tags into our terminal symbols as it is usually done (Klein and Manning, 2004; Bod, 2006a).

We start by finding the best independent set. To solve the problem in the practice, we convert it into an Integer Linear Programming (ILP) problem. ILP is also NP-hard (Karp, 1972), but there is software that implements efficient strategies for solving some of its instances (Achterberg, 2004).

ILP problems are defined by three parameters. First, there is a set of variables that can take values from a finite set. Second, there is an objective function that has to be maximized, and third, there is a set of constraints that must be satisfied. In our case, we define a binary variable $x_s \in \{0, 1\}$ for every node s in the graph. Its value is 1 or 0, that respectively determines the presence or absence of s in the set C_{max}. The objective function is

$$\sum_{s \in S(L)} x_s w(s)$$

The constraints are defined using the edges of the

graph. For every edge (s_1, s_2) in the graph, we add the following constraint to the problem:

$$x_{s_1} + x_{s_2} \leq 1$$

The 7422 trees of the WSJ10 treebank have a total of 181476 substrings of length ≥ 2, that form the set $S(L)$ of 68803 different substrings. The number of substrings in $S(L)$ does not grow too much with respect to the number of strings in L because substrings are sequences of POS tags, meaning that each substring is very frequent in the corpus. If substrings were made out of words instead of POS tags, the number of substrings would grow much faster, making the problem harder to solve. Moreover, removing the strings s such that $w(s) \leq 0$ gives a total of only 7029 substrings. Since there is a node for each substring, the resulting graph contains 7029 nodes. Recall that there is an edge between two strings if they occur overlapped. Our graph contains 1204 edges. The ILP version has 7029 variables, 1204 constraints and the objective function sums over 7029 variables. These numbers are summarized in Table 1.

The solution of the ILP problem is a set of 6583 variables that are set to one. This set corresponds to a set C_{max} of nodes in our graph of the same number of elements. Using C_{max} we build a new version T_{max} of the WSJ10, and compute its weight W, precision, recall and $F1$. Their values are displayed in Table 2. Since the elements of L were not introduced in $S(L)$, elements of L are not necessarily in C_{max}, but in order to compute precision and recall, we add them by hand. Strictly speaking, the set of constituents that we use for building T_{max} is C_{max} plus the full span brackets.

We can, using equation (2), compute the upper bound of $F1$ for all the possible scores of all UNTS grammars that use POS tags as alphabet:

$$f(w_{max}) = F1\left(\frac{1}{2 - \frac{w_{max}}{K}}, 1\right) = 82.2\%$$

The precision for this upper bound is

$$P(w_{max}) = \frac{1}{2 - \frac{w_{max}}{K}} = 69.8\%$$

while its recall is $R = 100\%$. Note from the previous section that $P(w_{max})$ is not an upper bound for precision but just the precision associated to the upper bound $f(w_{max})$.

Gold constituents	K	35302
Strings	$\|S(L)\|$	68803
Nodes		7029
Edges		1204

Table 1: Figures for the WSJ10 and its graph.

Hits	H	22169
Misses	M	2127
Weight	W	20042
Precision	P	91.2%
Recall	R	62.8%
F1	$F1$	74.4%

Table 2: Summary of the scores for C_{max}.

Table 3 shows results that allow us to compare the upper bounds with state-of-the-art parsing scores. BestW corresponds to the scores of T_{max} and UBoundF1 is the result of our translation function f. From the table we can see that an unsupervised parser based on UNTS grammars may reach a sate-of-the-art performance over the WSJ10. RBranch is a WSJ10 version where all trees are binary and right branching. DMV, CCM and DMV+CCM are the results reported in Klein and Manning (2004). U-DOP and UML-DOP are the results reported in Bod (2006b) and Bod (2006a) respectively. Incremental refers to the results reported in Seginer (2007).

We believe that our upper bound is a generous one and that it might be difficult to achieve it for two reasons. First, since the WSJ10 corpus is a rather flat treebank, from the 68803 substrings only 10% of them are such that $c(s) > d(s)$. Our procedure has to decide among this 10% which of the strings are constituents. An unsupervised method has to choose the set of constituents from the set of all 68803 possible substrings. Second, we are supposing a recall of 100% which is clearly too optimistic. We believe that we can find a tighter upper bound by finding an upper bound for recall, and by rewriting f in equation (2) in terms of the upper bound for recall.

It must be clear the scope of the upper bound we found. First, note that it has been computed over the WSJ10 treebank using the POS tags as the alphabet. Any other alphabet we use, like for example words, or pairs of words and POS tags, changes the relation of compatibility among the substrings, making a completely different universe

Model	UP	UR	F1
RBranch	55.1	70.0	61.7
DMV	46.6	59.2	52.1
CCM	64.2	81.6	71.9
DMV+CCM	69.3	88.0	77.6
U-DOP	70.8	88.2	78.5
UML-DOP			82.9
Incremental	75.6	76.2	75.9
BestW(UNTS)	91.2	62.8	**74.4**
UBoundF1(UNTS)	69.8	100.0	**82.2**

Table 3: Performance on the WSJ10 of the most recent unsupervised parsers, and our upper bounds on UNTS.

of UNTS grammars. Second, our computation of the upper bound was not made for supersets of the WSJ10. Supersets such as the entire Penn Treebank produce bigger graphs because they contain longer sentences and various different sequences of substrings. As the maximization of W is an NP-hard problem, the computational cost of solving bigger instances grows exponentially. A third limitation that must be clear is about the models affected by the bound. The upper bound, and in general the method, is only applicable to the class of formal UNTS grammars, with only some very slight variants mentioned in the previous sections. Just moving to probabilistic or weighted UNTS grammars invalidates all the presented results.

6 Conclusions

We present a method for assessing the potential of UNTS grammars as a formalism for unsupervised parsing of natural language. We assess their potential by finding an upper bound of their performance when they are evaluated using the WSJ10 treebank. We show that any UNTS grammars can achieve at most 82.2% of $F1$ measure, a value comparable to most state-of-the-art models. In order to compute this upper bound we introduced a measure that does not define the same ordering among UNTS grammars as the $F1$, but that has the advantage of being computationally easier to optimize. Our measure can be used, by means of a translation function, to find an upper bound for $F1$. We also showed that the optimization procedure for our metric maps into an NP-Hard problem, but despite this fact we present experimental results that compute the upper bound for the WSJ10 when POS tags are treated as the grammar alphabet.

From a more abstract perspective, we introduced a different approach to assess the usefulness of a grammatical formalism. Usually, formalism are proved to have interesting learnability properties such as PAC-learnability or convergence of a probabilistic distribution. We present an approach that even though it does not provide an effective way of computing the best grammar in an unsupervised fashion, it states the upper bound of performance for all the class of UNTS grammars.

Acknowledgments

This work was supported in part by grant PICT 2006-00969, ANPCyT, Argentina. We would like to thank Pablo Rey (UDP, Chile) for his help with ILP, and Demetrio Martín Vilela (UNC, Argentina) for his detailed review.

References

Tobias Achterberg. 2004. SCIP - a framework to integrate Constraint and Mixed Integer Programming. Technical report.

Rens Bod. 2006a. An all-subtrees approach to unsupervised parsing. In *Proceedings of COLING-ACL 2006*.

Rens Bod. 2006b. Unsupervised parsing with U-DOP. In *Proceedings of CoNLL-X*.

Alexander Clark. 2006. PAC-learning unambiguous NTS languages. In *Proceedings of ICGI-2006*.

Alexander Clark. 2007. Learning deterministic context free grammars: The Omphalos competition. *Machine Learning*, 66(1):93–110.

Richard M. Karp. 1972. Reducibility among combinatorial problems. In R. E. Miller and J. W. Thatcher, editors, *Complexity of Computer Computations*, pages 85–103. Plenum Press.

Dan Klein and Christopher D. Manning. 2004. Corpus-based induction of syntactic structure: Models of dependency and constituency. In *Proceedings of ACL 42*.

Mitchell P. Marcus, Beatrice Santorini, and Mary A. Marcinkiewicz. 1994. Building a large annotated corpus of english: The Penn treebank. *Computational Linguistics*, 19(2):313–330.

Yoav Seginer. 2007. Fast unsupervised incremental parsing. In *Proceedings of ACL 45*.

Comparing learners for Boolean partitions: implications for morphological paradigms *

Katya Pertsova
University of North Carolina,
Chapel Hill
pertsova@email.unc.edu

Abstract

In this paper, I show that a problem of learning a morphological paradigm is similar to a problem of learning a partition of the space of Boolean functions. I describe several learners that solve this problem in different ways, and compare their basic properties.

1 Introduction

Lately, there has been a lot of work on acquiring paradigms as part of the word-segmentation problem (Zeman, 2007; Goldsmith, 2001; Snover et al., 2002). However, the problem of learning the distribution of affixes within paradigms as a function of their semantic (or syntactic) features is much less explored to my knowledge. This problem can be described as follows: suppose that the segmentation has already been established. Can we now predict what affixes should appear in what contexts, where by a 'context' I mean something quite general: some specification of semantic (and/or syntactic) features of the utterance. For example, one might say that the nominal suffix -z in English (as in *apple-z*) occurs in contexts that involve plural or possesive nouns whose stems end in a voiced segment.

In this paper, I show that the problem of learning the distribution of morphemes in contexts specified over some finite number of features is roughly equivalent to the problem of learning Boolean partitions of DNF formulas. Given this insight, one can easily extend standard DNF-learners to morphological paradigm learners. I show how this can be done on an example of the classical k-DNF learner (Valiant, 1984). This insight also allows us to bridge the paradigm-learning problem with other similar problems in the domain of cognitive science for which DNF's have been used, e.g., concept learning. I also describe two other learners proposed specifically for learning morphological paradigms. The first of these learners, proposed by me, was designed to capture certain empirical facts about syncretism and free variation in typological data (Pertsova, 2007). The second learner, proposed by David Adger, was designed as a possible explanation of another empirical fact - uneven frequencies of free variants in paradigms (Adger, 2006).

In the last section, I compare the learners on some simple examples and comment on their merits and the key differences among the algorithms. I also draw connections to other work, and discuss directions for further empirical tests of these proposals.

2 The problem

Consider a problem of learning the distribution of inflectional morphemes as a function of some set of features. Using featural representations, we can represent morpheme distributions in terms of a formula. The DNF formulas are commonly used for such algebraic representation. For instance, given the nominal suffix -z mentioned in the introduction, we can assign to it the following representation: $[(noun; +voiced]_{stem}; +plural) \vee (noun; +voiced]_{stem}; +possesive)]$. Presumably, features like $[plural]$ or [+*voiced*] or $]_{stem}$ (end of the stem) are accessible to the learners' cognitive system, and can be exploited during the learning process for the purpose of "grounding" the distribution of morphemes.[1] This way of looking at things is similar to how some researchers conceive of concept-learning or word-

*This paper ows a great deal to the input from Ed Stabler. As usual, all the errors and shortcomings are entirely mine.

[1]Assuming an a priori given universal feature set, the problem of feature discovery is a subproblem of learning morpheme distributions. This is because learning what feature condition the distribution is the same as learning what features (from the universal set) are relevant and should be paid attention to.

Proceedings of the EACL 2009 Workshop on Computational Linguistic Aspects of Grammatical Inference, pages 66–74,
Athens, Greece, 30 March 2009.

learning (Siskind, 1996; Feldman, 2000; Nosofsky et al., 1994).

However, one prominent distinction that sets inflectional morphemes apart from words is that they occur in paradigms, semantic spaces defining a relatively small set of possible distinctions. In the absence of free variation, one can say that the affixes define a partition of this semantic space into disjoint blocks, in which each block is associated with a unique form. Consider for instance a present tense paradigm of the verb "to be" in standard English represented below as a partition of the set of environments over the following features: *class* (with values *masc, fem, both (masc & fem),inanim,*), *number* (with values $+sg$ and $-sg$), and *person* (with values *1st, 2nd, 3rd*).[2]

am	1st. person; fem; +sg.
	1st. person; masc; +sg.
are	2nd. person; fem; +sg.
	2nd. person; masc; +sg.
	2nd. person; fem; −sg.
	2nd. person; masc; −sg.
	2nd. person; both; −sg.
	1st. person; fem; −sg.
	1st. person; masc; −sg.
	1st. person; both; −sg.
	3rd. person; masc; −sg
	3rd. person; fem; −sg
	3rd. person; both; −sg
	3rd. person; inanim; −sg
is	3rd person; masc; +sg
	3rd person; fem; +sg
	3rd person; inanim; +sg

Each block in the above partition can be represented as a mapping between the phonological form of the morpheme (a *morph*) and a DNF formula. A single morph will be typically mapped to a DNF containing a single conjunction of features (called a *monomial*). When a morph is mapped to a disjunction of monomials (as the morph [-z] discussed above), we think of such a morph as a homonym (having more than one "meaning"). Thus, one way of defining the learning problem is in terms of learning a partition of a set of DNF's.

[2]These particular features and their values are chosen just for illustration. There might be a much better way to represent the distinctions encoded by the pronouns. Also notice that the feature values are not fully independent: some combinations are logically ruled out (e.g. speakers and listeners are usually animate entities).

Alternatively, we could say that the learner has to learn a partition of Boolean functions associated with each morph (a Boolean function for a morph m maps the contexts in which m occurs to $true$, and all other contexts to $false$).

However, when paradigms contain free variation, the divisions created by the morphs no longer define a partition since a single context may be associated with more than one morph. (Free variation is attested in world's languages, although it is rather marginal (Kroch, 1994).) In case a paradigm contains free variation, it is still possible to represent it as a partition by doing the following:

(1) Take a singleton partition of morph-meaning pairs (m, r) and merge any cells that have the same meaning r. Then merge those blocks that are associated with the same set of morphs.

Below is an example of how we can use this trick to partition a paradigm with free-variation. The data comes from the past tense forms of "to be" in Buckie English.

was	1st. person; fem; +sg.
	1st. person; masc; +sg.
	3rd person; masc; +sg
	3rd person; fem; +sg
	3rd person; inanim; +sg
was/were	2nd. person; fem; +sg.
	2nd. person; masc; +sg.
	2nd. person; fem; −sg.
	2nd. person; masc; −sg.
	2nd. person; both; −sg.
	1st. person; fem; −sg.
	1st. person; masc; −sg.
	1st. person; both; −sg.
were	3rd. person; masc; −sg
	3rd. person; fem; −sg
	3rd. person; both; −sg
	3rd. person; inanim; −sg

In general, then, the problem of learning the distribution of morphs within a single inflectional paradigm is equivalent to learning a Boolean partition.

In what follows, I consider and compare several learners for learning Boolean partitions. Some of these learners are extensions of learners proposed in the literature for learning DNFs. Other learners were explicitly proposed for learning morphological paradigms.

We should keep in mind that all these learners are idealizations and are not realistic if only because they are batch-learners. However, because they are relatively simple to state and to understand, they allow a deeper understanding of what properties of the data drive generalization.

2.1 Some definitions

Assume a finite set of morphs, Σ, and a finite set of features F. It would be convenient to think of morphs as chunks of phonological material corresponding to the pronounced morphemes.[3] Every feature $f \in F$ is associated with some set of values V_f that includes a value $[*]$, unspecified. Let S be the space of all possible complete assignments over F (an assignment is a set $\{f_i \rightarrow V_f | \forall f_i \in F\}$). We will call those assignments that do not include any unspecified features *environments*. Let the set $S' \subseteq S$ correspond to the set of environments.

It should be easy to see that the set S forms a Boolean lattice with the following relation among the assignments, $\leq_R$: for any two assignments a_1 and a_2, $a_1 \leq_R a_2$ iff the value of every feature f_i in a_1 is identical to the value of f_i in a_2, unless f_i is unspecified in a_2. The top element of the lattice is an assignment in which all features are unspecified, and the bottom is the contradiction. Every element of the lattice is a *monomial* corresponding to the conjunction of the specified feature values. An example lattice for two binary features is given in Figure 1.

Figure 1: A lattice for 2 binary features

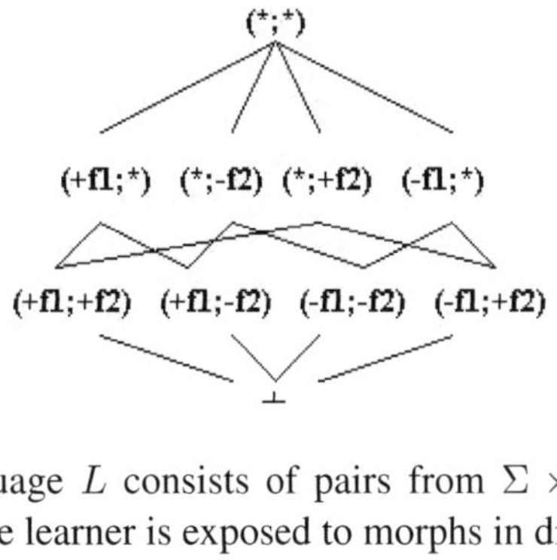

A language L consists of pairs from $\Sigma \times S'$. That is, the learner is exposed to morphs in different environments.

One way of stating the learning problem is to say that the learner has to learn a grammar for the target language L (we would then have to specify what this grammar should look like). Another way is to say that the learner has to learn the language mapping itself. We can do the latter by using Boolean functions to represent the mapping of each morph to a set of environments. Depending on how we state the learning problem, we might get different results. For instance, it's known that some subsets of DNF's are not learnable, while the Boolean functions corresponding to them are learnable (Valiant, 1984). Since I will use Boolean functions for some of the learners below, I introduce the following notation. Let B be the set of Boolean functions mapping elements of S' to *true* or *false*. For convenience, we say that b_m corresponds to a Boolean function that maps a set of environments to *true* when they are associated with m in L, and to *false* otherwise.

3 Learning Algorithms

3.1 Learner 1: an extension of the Valiant k-DNF learner

An observation that a morphological paradigm can be represented as a partition of environments in which each block corresponds to a mapping between a morph and a DNF, allows us to easily convert standard DNF learning algorithms that rely on positive and negative examples into paradigm-learning algorithms that rely on positive examples only. We can do that by iteratively applying any DNF learning algorithm treating instances of input pairs like (m, e) as positive examples for m and as negative examples for all other morphs.

Below, I show how this can be done by extending a k-DNF[4] learner of (Valiant, 1984) to a paradigm-learner. To handle cases of free variation we need to keep track of what morphs occur in exactly the same environments. We can do this by defining the partition Π on the input following the recipe in (1) (substituting environments for the variable r).

The original learner learns from negative examples alone. It initializes the hypothesis to the disjunction of all possible conjunctions of length at most k, and subtracts from this hypothesis monomials that are consistent with the negative examples. We will do the same thing for each

[3] However, we could also conceive of morphs as functions specifying what transformations apply to the stem without much change to the formalism.

[4] k-DNF formula is a formula with at most k feature values in each conjunct.

morph using positive examples only (as described above), and forgoing subtraction in a cases of free-variation. The modified learner is given below. The following additional notation is used: Lex is the lexicon or a hypothesis. The formula D is a disjunction of all possible conjunctions of length at most k. We say that two assignments are *consistent* with each other if they agree on all specified features. Following standard notation, we assume that the learner is exposed to some text T that consists of an infinite sequence of (possibly) repeating elements from L. t_j is a finite subsequence of the first j elements from T. $L(t_j)$ is the set of elements in t_j.

Learner 1 (input: t_j)

1. set $Lex := \{\langle m, D\rangle | \; \exists\langle m, e\rangle \in L(t_j)\}$
2. For each $\langle m, e\rangle \in L(t_j)$, for each m' s.t. $\neg\exists$ block $bl \in \Pi$ of $L(t_j)$, $\langle m, e\rangle \in bl$ and $\langle m', e\rangle \in bl$: replace $\langle m', f\rangle$ in Lex by $\langle m', f'\rangle$ where f' is the result of removing every monomial consistent with e.

This learner initially assumes that every morph can be used everywhere. Then, when it hears one morph in a given environment, it assumes that no other morph can be heard in exactly that environment unless it already knows that this environment permits free variation (this is established in the partition Π).

4 Learner 2:

The next learner is an elaboration on the previous learner. It differs from it in only one respect: instead of initializing lexical representations of every morph to be a disjunction of all possible monomials of length at most k, we initialize it to be the disjunction of all and only those monomials that are consistent with some environment paired with the morph in the language. This learner is similar to the DNF learners that do something on both positive and negative examples (see (Kushilevitz and Roth, 1996; Blum, 1992)).

So, for every morph m used in the language, we define a disjunction of monomials D_m that can be derived as follows. (i) Let E_m be the enumeration of all environments in which m occurs in L (ii) let M_i correspond to a set of all subsets of feature values in e_i, $e_i \in E$ (iii) let D_m be $\bigvee M$, where a set $s \in M$ iff $s \in M_i$, for some i.

Learner 2 can now be stated as a learner that is identical to Learner 1 except for the initial setting of Lex. Now, Lex will be set to $Lex := \{\langle m, D_m\rangle | \; \exists\langle m, e\rangle \in L(t_i)\}$.

Because this learner does not require enumeration of all possible monomials, but just those that are consistent with the positive data, it can handle "polynomially explainable" subclass of DNF's (for more on this see (Kushilevitz and Roth, 1996)).

5 Learner 3: a learner biased towards monomial and elsewhere distributions

Next, I present a batch version of a learner I proposed based on certain typological observations and linguists' insights about blocking. The typological observations come from a sample of verbal agreement paradigms (Pertsova, 2007) and personal pronoun paradigms (Cysouw, 2003) showing that majority of paradigms have either "monomial" or "elsewhere" distribution (defined below).

Roughly speaking, a morph has a monomial distribution if it can be described with a single monomial. A morph has an elsewhere distribution if this distribution can be viewed as a complement of distributions of other monomial or elsewhere-morphs. To define these terms more precisely I need to introduce some additional notation. Let $\bigcap e_x$ be the intersection of all environments in which morph x occurs (i.e., these are the invariant features of x). This set corresponds to a least upper bound of the environments associated with x in the lattice $\langle S, \leq_R\rangle$, call it lub_x. Then, let the *minimal monomial function* for a morph x, denoted mm_x, be a Boolean function that maps an environment to $true$ if it is consistent with lub_x and to $false$ otherwise. As usual, an extension of a Boolean function, $ext(b)$ is the set of all assignments that b maps to true.

(2) Monomial distribution
A morph x has a monomial distribution iff $b_x \equiv mm_x$.

The above definition states that a morph has a monomial distribution if its invariant features pick out just those environments that are associated with this morph in the language. More concretely, if a monomial morph always co-occurs with the feature *+singular*, it will appear in *all* singular environments in the language.

(3) Elsewhere distribution
A morph x has an elsewhere distribution iff $b_x \equiv mm_x - (mm_{x_1} \vee mm_{x_2} \vee \ldots \vee (mm_{x_n}))$ for all $x_i \neq x$ in Σ.

The definition above amounts to saying that a morph has an elsewhere distribution if the environments in which it occurs are in the extension of its minimal monomial function minus the minimal monomial functions of all other morphs. An example of a lexical item with an elsewhere distribution is the present tense form *are* of the verb "to be", shown below.

Table 1: The present tense of "to be" in English

	sg.	pl
1p.	am	are
2p.	are	are
3p.	is	are

Elsewhere morphemes are often described in linguistic accounts by appealing to the notion of blocking. For instance, the lexical representation of *are* is said to be unspecified for both person and number, and is said to be "blocked" by two other forms: *am* and *is*. My hypothesis is that the reason why such non-monotonic analyses appear so natural to linguists is the same reason for why monomial and elsewhere distributions are typologically common: namely, the learners (and, apparently, the analysts) are prone to generalize the distribution of morphs to minimal monomials first, and later correct any overgeneralizations that might arise by using default reasoning, i.e. by positing exceptions that override the general rule. Of course, the above strategy alone is not sufficient to capture distributions that are neither monomial, nor elsewhere (I call such distributions "overlapping", cf. the suffixes *-en* and *-t* in the German paradigm in Table 2), which might also explain why such paradigms are typologically rare.

Table 2: Present tense of some regular verbs in German

	sg.	pl
1p.	-e	-en
2p.	-st	-t
3p.	-t	-en

The original learner I proposed is an incremental learner that calculates grammars similar to those proposed by linguists, namely grammars consisting of a lexicon and a filtering "blocking" component. The version presented here is a simpler batch learner that learns a partition of Boolean functions instead.[5] Nevertheless, the main properties of the original learner are preserved: specifically, a bias towards monomial and elsewhere distributions.

To determine what kind of distribution a morph has, I define a relation C. A morph m stands in a relation C to another morph m' if $\exists\langle m, e\rangle \in L$, such that $lub_{m'}$ is consistent with e. In other words, mCm' if m occurs in any environment consistent with the invariant features of m'. Let C^+ be a transitive closure of C.

Learner 3 (input: t_j)

1. Let $S(t_j)$ be the set of pairs in t_j containing monomial- or elsewhere-distribution morphs. That is, $\langle m, e\rangle \in S(t_j)$ iff $\neg\exists m'$ such that mC^+m' and $m'C^+m$.

2. Let $O(t_j) = t_j - S(t_j)$ (the set of all other pairs).

3. A pair $\langle m, e\rangle \in S$ is a *least element* of S iff $\neg\exists\langle m', e'\rangle \in (S - \{\langle m, e\rangle\})$ such that $m'C^+m$.

4. Given a hypothesis Lex, and for any expression $\langle m, e\rangle \in Lex$: let $rem((m, e), Lex) = (m, (mm_m - \{b|\langle m', b\rangle \in Lex\}))$[6]

> 1. set $S := S(t_j)$ and $Lex := \emptyset$
>
> 2. While $S \neq \emptyset$: remove a *least* x from S and set $Lex := Lex \cup rem(x, Lex)$
>
> 3. Set $Lex := Lex \cup O(t_j)$.

This learner initially assumes that the lexicon is empty. Then it proceeds adding Boolean functions corresponding to minimal monomials for morphs that are in the set $S(t_j)$ (i.e., morphs that have either monomial or elsewhere distributions). This

[5] I thank Ed Stabler for relating this batch learner to me (p.c.).

[6] For any two Boolean functions b, b': $b - b'$ is the function that maps e to 1 iff $e \in ext(b)$ and $e \notin ext(b')$. Similarly, $b + b'$ is the function that maps e to 1 iff $e \in ext(b)$ and $e \in ext(b')$.

is done in a particular order, namely in the order in which the morphs can be said to block each other. The remaining text is learned by rote-memorization. Although this learner is more complex than the previous two learners, it generalizes fast when applied to paradigms with monomial and elsewhere distributions.

5.1 Learner 4: a learner biased towards shorter formulas

Next, I discuss a learner for morphological paradigms, proposed by another linguist, David Adger. Adger describes his learner informally showing how it would work on a few examples. Below, I formalize his proposal in terms of learning Boolean partitions. The general strategy of this learner is to consider simplest monomials first (those with the fewer number of specified features) and see how much data they can unambiguously and non-redundantly account for. If a monomial is consistent with several morphs in the text - it is discarded unless the morphs in question are in free variation. This simple strategy is reiterated for the next set of most simple monomials, etc.

Learner 4 (input t_j)

1. Let M_i be the set of all monomials over F with i specified features.

2. Let B_i be the set of Boolean functions from environments to truth values corresponding to M_i in the following way: for each monomial $mn \in M_i$ the corresponding Boolean function b is such that $b(e) = 1$ if e is an environment consistent with mn; otherwise $b(e) = 0$.

3. Uniqueness check:
   For a Boolean function b, morph m, and text t_j let $unique(b, m, t_j) = 1$ iff $ext(b_m) \subseteq ext(b)$ and $\neg\exists\langle m', e\rangle \in L(t_j)$, s.t. $e \in ext(b)$ and $e \notin ext(b_m)$.

> 1. set $Lex := \Sigma \times \emptyset$ and $i := 0$;
>
> 2. while Lex does not correspond to $L(t_j)$ AND $i \leq |F|$ do:
>   for each $b \in B_i$, for each m, s.t. $\exists\langle m, e\rangle \in L(t_j)$:
>
>   - if $unique(b, m, t_j) = 1$ then replace $\langle m, f\rangle$ with $\langle m, f + b\rangle$ in Lex
>
> $i \leftarrow i + 1$

This learner considers all monomials in the order of their simplicity (determined by the number of specified features), and if the monomial in question is consistent with environments associated with a unique morph then these environments are added to the extension of the Boolean function for that morph. As a result, this learner will converge faster on paradigms in which morphs can be described with disjunctions of shorter monomials since such monomials are considered first.

6 Comparison

6.1 Basic properties

First, consider some of the basic properties of the learners presented here. For this purpose, we will assume that we can apply these learners in an iterative fashion to larger and larger batches of data. We say that a learner is *consistent* if and only if, given a text t_j, it always converges on the grammar generating all the data seen in t_j (Osherson et al., 1986). A learner is *monotonic* if and only if for every text t and every point $j < k$, the hypothesis the learner converges on at t_j is a subset of the hypothesis at t_k (or for learners that learn by elimination: the hypothesis at t_j is a superset of the hypothesis at t_k). And, finally, a learner is *generalizing* if and only if for some t_j it converges on a hypothesis that makes a prediction beyond the elements of t_j.

The table below classifies the four learners according to the above properties.

Learner	consist.	monoton.	generalizing
Learner 1	yes	yes	yes
Learner 2	yes	yes	yes
Learner 3	yes	no	yes
Learner 4	yes	yes	yes

All learners considered here are generalizing and consistent, but they differ with respect to monotonicity. Learner 3 is non-monotonic while the remaining learners are monotonic. While monotonicity is a nice computational property, some aspects of human language acquisition are suggestive of a non-monotonic learning strategy, e.g. the presence of overgeneralization errors and their subsequent corrections by children(Marcus et al., 1992). Thus, the fact that Learner 3 is non-monotonic might speak in its favor.

6.2 Illustration

To demonstrate how the learners work, consider this simple example. Suppose we are learning the following distribution of morphs A and B over 2 binary features.

(4) Example 1

	+f1	−f1
+f2	A	B
−f2	B	B

Suppose further that the text t_3 is:

A $+f1; +f2$
B $-f1; +f2$
B $+f1; -f2$

Learner 1 generalizes right away by assuming that every morph can appear in every environment which leads to massive overgeneralizations. These overgeneralizations are eventually eliminated as more data is discovered. For instance, after processing the first pair in the text above, the learner "learns" that B does not occur in any environment consistent with $(+f1; +f2)$ since it has just seen A in that environment. After processing t_3, Learner 1 has the following hypothesis:

A $(+f1; +f2) \vee (-f1; -f2)$
B $(-f1) \vee (-f2)$

That is, after seeing t_3, Learner 2 correctly predicts the distribution of morphs in environments that it has seen, but it still predicts that both A and B should occur in the not-yet-observed environment, $(-f1; -f2)$. This learner can sometimes converge before seeing all data-points, especially if the input includes a lot of free variation. If fact, if in the above example A and B were in free variation in all environments, Learner 1 would have converged right away on its initial setting of the lexicon. However, in paradigms with no free variation convergence is typically slow since the learner follows a very conservative strategy of learning by elimination.

Unlike Learner 1, Learner 2 will converge after seeing t_3. This is because this learner's initial hypothesis is more restricted. Namely, the initial hypothesis for A includes disjunction of only those monomials that are consistent with $(+f1; +f2)$. Hence, A is never overgeneralized to $(-f1; -f2)$. Like Learner 1, Learner 2 also learns by elimination, however, on top of that it also restricts its initial hypothesis which leads to faster convergence.

Let's now consider the behavior of learner 3 on example 1. Recall that this learner first computes minimal monomials of all morphs, and checks in they have monomial or elsewhere distributions (this is done via the relation C^+). In this case, A has a monomial distribution, and B has an elsewhere distribution. Therefore, the learner first computes the Boolean function for A whose extension is simply $(+f1; +f2)$; and then the Boolean function for B, whose extension includes environments consistent with (*;*) minus those consistent with $(+f1; +f2)$, which yields the following hypothesis:

$ext(b_A)$ $[+f1; +f2]$
$ext(b_B)$ $[-f1; +f2][+f1; -f2][-f1; -f2]$

That is, Learner 3 generalizes and converges on the right language after seeing text t_3.

Learner 4 also converges at this point. This learner first considers how much data can be unambiguously accounted for with the most minimal monomial (*;*). Since both A and B occur in environments consistent with this monomial, nothing is added to the lexicon. On the next round, it considers all monomials with one specified feature. 2 such monomials, $(-f1)$ and $(-f2)$, are consistent only with B, and so we predict B to appear in the not-yet-seen environment $(-f1; -f2)$. Thus, the hypothesis that Learner 4 arrives at is the same as the hypothesis Learners 3 arrives at after seeing t_3.

6.3 Differences

While the last three learners perform similarly on the simple example above, there are significant differences between them. These differences become apparent when we consider larger paradigms with homonymy and free variation.

First, let's look at an example that involves a more elaborate homonymy than example 1. Consider, for instance, the following text.

(5) Example 2

A $[+f1; +f2; +f3]$
A $[+f1; -f2; -f3]$
A $[+f1; +f2; -f3]$
A $[-f1; +f2; +f3]$
B $[-f1; -f2; -f3]$

Given this text, all three learners will differ in their predictions with respect to the environment $(-f1; +f2; -f3)$. Learner 2 will predict both A and B to occur in this environment since not enough monomials will be removed from representations of A or B to rule out either morph from occurring in $(-f1; +f2; -f3)$. Learner 3 will predict A to appear in all environments that haven't been seen yet, including $(-f1; +f2; -f3)$. This is because in the current text the minimal monomial for A is $(*; *; *)$ and A has an elsewhere distribution. On the other hand, Learner 4 predicts B to occur in $(-f1; +f2; -f3)$. This is because the extension of the Boolean function for B includes any environments consistent with $(-f1; -f3)$ or $(-f1; -f2)$ since these are the simplest monomials that uniquely pick out B.

Thus, the three learners follow very different generalization routes. Overall, Learner 2 is more cautious and slower to generalize. It predicts free variation in all environments for which not enough data has been seen to converge on a single morph. Learner 3 is unique in preferring monomial and elsewhere distributions. For instance, in the above example it treats A as a 'default' morph. Learner 4 is unique in its preference for morphs describable with disjunction of simpler monomials. Because of this preference, it will sometimes generalize even after seeing just one instance of a morph (since several simple monomials can be consistent with this instance alone).

One way to test what the human learners do in a situation like the one above is to use artificial grammar learning experiments. Such experiments have been used for learning individual concepts over features like shape, color, texture, etc. Some work on concept learning suggests that it is subjectively easier to learn concepts describable with shorter formulas (Feldman, 2000; Feldman, 2004). Other recent work challenges this idea (Lafond et al., 2007), showing that people don't always converge on the most minimal representation, but instead go for the more simple and general representation and learn exceptions to it (this approach is more in line with Learner 3).

Some initial results from my pilot experiments on learning partitions of concept spaces (using abstract shapes, rather than language stimuli) also suggest that people find paradigms with elsewhere distributions easier to learn than the ones with overlapping distributions (like the German paradigms in 2). However, I also found a bias toward paradigms with the fewer number of relevant features. This bias is consistent with Learner 4 since this learner tries to assume the smallest number of relevant features possible. Thus, both learners have their merits.

Another area in which the considered learners make somewhat different predictions has to do with free variation. While I can't discuss this at length due to space constraints, let me comment that any batch learner can easily detect free-variation before generalizing, which is exactly what most of the above learners do (except Learner 3, but it can also be changed to do the same thing). However, since free variation is rather marginal in morphological paradigms, it is possible that it would be rather problematic. In fact, free variation is more problematic if we switch from the batch learners to incremental learners.

7 Directions for further research

There are of course many other learners one could consider for learning paradigms, including approaches quite different in spirit from the ones considered here. In particular, some recently popular approaches conceive of learning as matching probabilities of the observed data (e.g., Bayesian learning). Comparing such approaches with the algorithmic ones is difficult since the criteria for success are defined so differently, but it would still be interesting to see whether the kinds of prior assumptions needed for a Bayesian model to match human performance would have something in common with properties that the learners considered here relied on. These properties include the disjoint nature of paradigm cells, the prevalence of monomial and elsewhere morphs, and the economy considerations. Other empirical work that might help to differentiate Boolean partition learners (besides typological and experimental work already mentioned) includes finding relevant language acquisition data, and examining (or modeling) language change (assuming that learning biases influence language change).

References

David Adger. 2006. Combinatorial variation. *Journal of Linguistics*, 42:503–530.

Avrim Blum. 1992. Learning Boolean functions in an infinite attribute space. *Machine Learning*, 9:373–386.

Michael Cysouw. 2003. *The Paradigmatic Structure of Person Marking*. Oxford University Press, NY.

Jacob Feldman. 2000. Minimization of complexity in human concept learning. *Nature*, 407:630–633.

Jacob Feldman. 2004. How surprising is a simple pattern? Quantifying 'Eureka!'. *Cognition*, 93:199–224.

John Goldsmith. 2001. Unsupervised learning of a morphology of a natural language. *Computational Linguistics*, 27:153–198.

Anthony Kroch. 1994. Morphosyntactic variation. In Katharine Beals et al., editor, *Papers from the 30th regional meeting of the Chicago Linguistics Society: Parasession on variation and linguistic theory*. Chicago Linguistics Society, Chicago.

Eyal Kushilevitz and Dan Roth. 1996. On learning visual concepts and DNF formulae. *Machine Learning*, 24:65–85.

Daniel Lafond, Yves Lacouture, and Guy Mineau. 2007. Complexity minimization in rule-based category learning: revising the catalog of boolean concepts and evidence for non-minimal rules. *Journal of Mathematical Psychology*, 51:57–74.

Gary Marcus, Steven Pinker, Michael Ullman, Michelle Hollander, T. John Rosen, and Fei Xu. 1992. Overregularization in language acquisition. *Monographs of the Society for Research in Child Development*, 57(4). Includes commentary by Harold Clahsen.

Robert M. Nosofsky, Thomas J. Palmeri, and S.C. McKinley. 1994. Rule-plus-exception model of classification learning. *Psychological Review*, 101:53–79.

Daniel Osherson, Scott Weinstein, and Michael Stob. 1986. *Systems that Learn*. MIT Press, Cambridge, Massachusetts.

Katya Pertsova. 2007. *Learning Form-Meaning Mappings in the Presence of Homonymy*. Ph.D. thesis, University of California, Los Angeles.

Jeffrey Mark Siskind. 1996. A computational study of cross-situational techniques for learning word-to-meaning mappings. *Cognition*, 61(1-2):1–38, Oct-Nov.

Matthew G. Snover, Gaja E. Jarosz, and Michael R. Brent. 2002. Unsupervised learning of morphology using a novel directed search algorithm: taking the first step. In *Proceedings of the ACL-02 workshop on Morphological and phonological learning*, pages 11–20, Morristown, NJ, USA. Association for Computational Linguistics.

Leslie G. Valiant. 1984. A theory of the learnable. *CACM*, 17(11):1134–1142.

Daniel Zeman. 2007. Unsupervised acquiring of morphological paradigms from tokenized text. In *Working Notes for the Cross Language Evaluation Forum*, Budapest. Madarsko. Workshop.